# Participatory planning
*for*
# integrated rural water supply *and* sanitation programmes

# Participatory planning

*for*

# integrated rural water supply *and* sanitation programmes:

## Guidelines and Manual

*Jeremy Ockelford & Bob Reed*

with contributions from

**Nick Robins, Mimi Khan, Jane Bañez-Ockelford,**

**Henry Gunston and Roger Calow**

Developed by:
WEDC
Water, Engineering and Development Centre, Loughborough University

British Geological Survey, Wallingford


Supported by:
Commonwealth Science Council, Commonwealth Secretariat, London


Funded by:
Department for International Development, London

**WEDC**

**BGS** 1835

Commonwealth Science Council

Water, Engineering and Development Centre,
Loughborough University,
Leicestershire, LE11 3TU, UK


© Water, Engineering and Development Centre Loughborough University 2006


ISBN 13 Paperback: 978 1 84380 098 9
ISBN Ebook: 9781788533157
Book DOI: http://dx.doi.org/10.3362/9781788533157

A catalogue record for this book is available from the British Library.

WEDC (The Water, Engineering and Development Centre) at Loughborough University in the UK is one of the world's leading institutions concerned with education, training, research and consultancy for the planning, provision and management of physical infrastructure for development in low- and middleincome countries.

This publication is also available on-line at:
http://wedc.lboro.ac.uk/publications/

Ockelford, J. and Reed, R.A. (2006)
Participatory Planning for Integrated Rural Water Supply and Sanitation Programmes (third edition)
WEDC, Loughborough University, UK.

This edition is reprinted and distributed by Practical Action Publishing.
Since 1974, Practical Action Publishing has published and disseminated books and information in support of international development work throughout the world. Practical Action Publishing trades only in support of its parent charity objectives and any profits are covenanted back to Practical Action (Charity Reg. No. 247257, Group VAT Registration No. 880 9924 76).

This document is an output from a project funded by the UK Department for International Development (DFID)
for the benefit of low-income countries.
The views expressed are not necessarily those of DFID.

# About the authors

**Jeremy Ockelford** is a civil engineer specialising in water supply and sanitation in developing countries. He has considerable experience in planning, management and evaluation of water supply and sanitation projects and programmes in Asia and Africa with governments, donors and NGOs. He is particularly interested in the interface between people and technology in the process of development, and in the institutional issues of governments, NGOs and communities working together. He works as an independent consultant based in London.

**Bob Reed** is a Senior Programme and Project Manager at the Water, Engineering and Development Centre. He specializes in water supply and sanitation for rural areas, low-income urban communities and refugees. He has considerable experience of training, design and project implementation in the Pacific, the Caribbean, Asia and Africa. In recent years he has focused on the provision of improved and sustainable water supply and sanitation systems for displaced populations.

The authors would like to hear from anyone who uses the guidelines in the field with comments on their usefulness and areas which require adaptation or improvement. Please forward comments or suggestions to Bob Reed at WEDC.

# The contributors

**Nick Robins** was a hydrogeologist with the British Geological Survey

**Mimi Khan** was a free lance Health Consultant working with water and sanitation in addition to a range of other international public health issues

**Jane Bañez-Ockelford** is a health professional with extensive experience in community development and participatory learning approaches.

**Henry Gunston** was a hydrologist with the Centre for Ecology and Hydrology

**Roger Calow** was a socio-economist with the British Geological Survey

# Acknowledgements

The authors would like to thank the following for the various contributions that they have made to the development of these *Guidelines and Manual*:

Siyan Malomo of the Commonwealth Secretariat in London, for his original idea, for his continued interest in and support of the project, and for making arrangements for the pilot studies.

Robin Herbert and Beatrice Gibbs, both formerly of BGS, for some early inputs into the concept of the guidelines.

Ian Smout of WEDC, for his constructive criticism and support.

For assistance and support in the First Pilot Study in Zimbabwe:
George Nhunhama and Benedict T. Majaya of the National Co-ordination Unit;
  Columbus Chimani, Solomon Makan'a and other members of the National Action Commit-
  tee;
  Members of the Provincial Water Supply & Sanitation Sub-Committee in Manicaland;
  Members of the Water Supply & Sanitation Sub-Committees in Nyanga and Makoni
  Districts.

For assistance and support in the Second Pilot Study in Zambia:
  Dennis Mwanza and other staff of the Reform Support Unit, Lusaka;
  Pola Kimena, Chimwang'a Maseka and Simon Kang'omba, Department of Water Affairs;
  S.T. Chisanga, Ministry of Health, Lusaka;
  Evaristo Makwaya, Ministry of Community Development & Social Affairs, Lusaka;
  Osward Mwansa and Vincent M. Nguluwe, Department of Water Affairs, Northern
  Province;
  Kayula Siame, Provincial Planning Unit, Northern Province;
  Officers of Luwingu, Chinsali and Isoka Districts;
  Participants of the Planning Workshop, from all the Districts of Northern Province.

Participants of the workshops at the 22nd WEDC Conference in New Delhi, India, and the 23rd WEDC Conference in Durban, South Africa, for discussions on the concept and content of the project.

The 1998, 1999, and 2000 M.Sc. students at WEDC, who practised some of the participatory planning methods for their water resource management module and provided some useful insights.

For reviewing the final draft of the *Guidelines* and providing constructive criticism and support, special thanks are due to:
  Bente Schiller, Royal Danish Ministry of Foreign Affairs
  Gerd Foerch, GTZ, Addis Ababa
  Paul Dean, Consultant

Kimberly Clarke, for editorial review of the *Guidelines*.

Finally, *maraming salamat* to Jane, for all her support, encouragement, ideas (particularly on community development issues and participatory methods), contributions and criticism, and especially for her patience.

'Every country has its own version of vegetable soup.'


From an unknown training manual on Culture and Development, quoted by Parimal Jha in the Foreword to *Fancy Footwork: Entrapment in and Coping with the Nepali Management Model,* Ivan Gyozo Somlai, 1992, published by Ratna Pustak Bhandar, Kathmandu.

# Contents

# Stage 2: Assessment and analysis

# List of flowcharts

# List of tables and figures

## Section A: Preparation Phase

### Guidelines

## Section B: Project to develop programme

### Guidelines

#### Stage 1: Information gathering, consultations and surveys

#### Stage 2: Assessment and analysis

# Introduction

## Background

The importance of integrating domestic water supply, hygiene practice and sanitation with community organisation, institutional management and other demands on water resources is well accepted. There is, however, a lack of guidance for professionals on how to achieve this integration. Many of the books that deal with water supply and sanitation concentrate on a particular subject and, although they may refer to related subjects, provide little help on how to combine them in a project.

To provide a solution to this problem, the Water, Engineering & Development Centre (WEDC) at Loughborough University and the British Geological Survey (BGS), with support from the Commonwealth Science Council (CSC) and funding from the British Department for International Development (DFID), have developed these Guidelines and Manual to help governments in the process of planning and designing integrated rural water supply and sanitation programmes.

## The purpose

The purpose is to improve the methodology and practice for the development of sustainable rural water supply and sanitation **programmes**. Although the Guidelines and Manual are intended for use for rural programmes, the approach can be adapted for peri-urban programmes.

Organisations such as the FAO, UNDP, and the World Bank have written books and guidelines to support policy and strategy development, and there are several books available on project development. The level that has been neglected is the support of programme development.

## Intended users

The Guidelines are to help planners and managers in national government departments to formulate programmes that organise and co-ordinate the activities of government departments, external support agencies, NGOs, and others working in domestic water supply and sanitation in the programme area. They can also be used by external consultants, and NGOs who could use the relevant parts for their own programmes.

## Definition of programme

There is much confusion in development circles between a 'project' and a 'programme', with the words often being used interchangeably. In a study of the literature various different definitions of programme were considered. A number of key words come out of these definitions: coherent, sector, geographical area, co-ordination, approach, activities, time, inter-related, procedure, framework.

The study also revealed opposing interpretations of the term 'programme'. On one side, a programme is a set of projects (sub-projects), each with its specific area, targets and time limits for control, which add up to bigger areas and targets and overall time limits. In other words, a programme is just a bigger more complex type of project, with the emphasis on implementation. On the other side, a programme is a coherent framework or co-ordinated approach to activities ranging from specific projects to policy development. The latter definition was considered the more appropriate for these Guidelines.

The Guidelines and Manual should help users to plan and design a programme, defined as:

**a coherent framework of procedures and activities for co-ordinating and regulating projects within the water and sanitation sector in a defined geographical area.**

## Approach

### Ownership
It has been realised that for many rural areas, successful operation and maintenance of water supply points by communities requires the communities themselves to 'own' them. This concept of ownership has been adapted to apply to the 'product' of the Guidelines and Manual. The Guidelines themselves are only a tool. The resulting product — the programme — must be 'owned' by the people who have used the tool to design it.

To try to achieve this ownership, the approach of the Guidelines is to question. As far as possible, the answers should come from the users. The Guidelines make suggestions as to what sort of information is needed, where to find it and how to use it, but the decisions have to be made by the planners and managers using the Guidelines.

### Integration
Integration of the various components of rural water supply and sanitation is essential. It is one of the fundamental goals of the Guidelines. To provide users with the information that will enable them to achieve integration, relationships between each of the major components is highlighted. A decision in one area is cross-referenced to another area. There are also complex inter-relationships between the components of the programme and the social, health, technical, economic, financial, institutional and environmental information that needs to be considered for each.

The Guidelines and Manual allow the users to take account of social, geographical and hydrogeological differences within the administrative areas by identifying such differences and suggesting location-specific variations for the programme.

## Document development
In June 1995, 36 governments endorsed a proposed project entitled 'Sustainable Rural Water Supply and Sanitation using Integrated Water Resource Management Principles' prepared by the Commonwealth Science Council. This evolved into a research and development project, 'Integrated Framework for Rural Water Supply and Sanitation in Groundwater Dependent Areas', which began in August 1996. The output from the project is these Guidelines and Manual.

This third edition contains broadly the same information as the first two editions but it is presented in a more useable format. The Manual part of the book is now provided electronically. This is because the Manual contains a large number of tables and charts that are meant to be completed during the design programme. Providing the information in electronic format allows the tables and charts to be 'live'. They can be extracted from the text and edited and used during the data gathering and analysis process. This not only makes the document as a whole more user friendly but reduces its size, making it easier to navigate. A complete copy of the Guidelines is also provided on the disc so that the whole document can be viewed electronically and selected parts printed as required.

### Participation in development
As far as possible, the developers consulted with potential users. This was done in several ways:

workshops, presentations and papers with discussion at international conferences, and pilot studies of the concept and the draft with host government departments. The main events were:

- workshops at conferences

  - 22nd WEDC Conference in New Delhi, September 1996
  - 23rd WEDC Conference in Durban, South Africa, September 1997
- poster presentation at the Community Water Supply & Sanitation Conference, World Bank, May 1998
- pilot studies of draft

  - 1st Pilot Study to test the concept with the National Co-ordination Unit in Zimbabwe, July and August, 1997
  - 2nd Pilot Study to field test draft guidelines by observed use by a government team, through the Water Sector Reform Support Unit in Zambia, June, July and August, and November, 1998

The final draft was also reviewed by, amongst others, representatives of two international development organisations.

# How to use the Guidelines and Manual

## Overview of the Programme Planning Process

The Guidelines are based on a standard programme cycle, as shown below. They help with Section A: Preparation Phase, and with Section B: Project to Develop Programme, which covers the first three stages of the cycle.

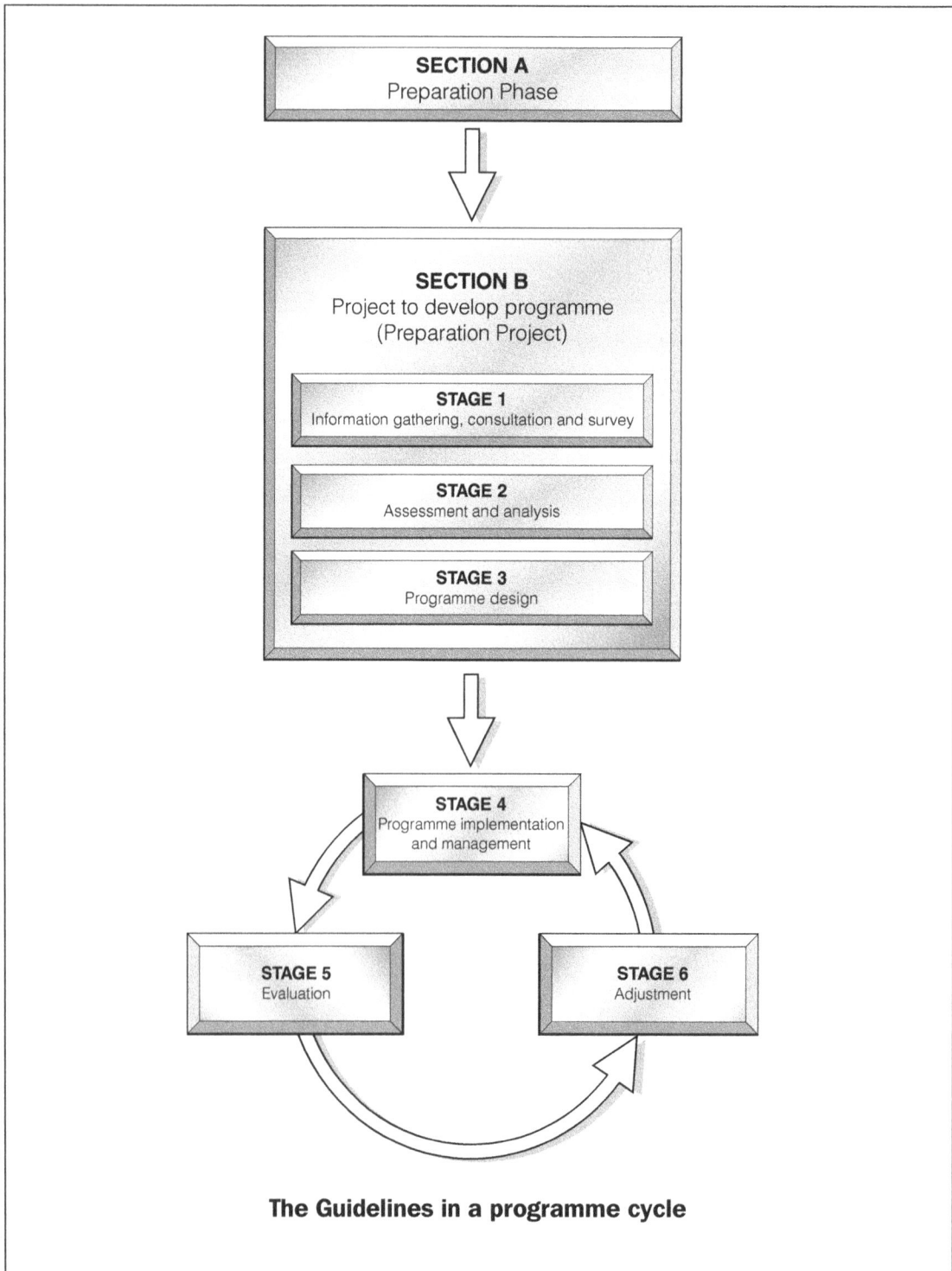

```
┌─────────────────────────────────────────────┐
│                                               │
│            ┌─────────────────────┐            │
│            │     SECTION A       │            │
│            │  Preparation Phase  │            │
│            └─────────────────────┘            │
│                      ▼                        │
│     ┌───────────────────────────────────┐     │
│     │            SECTION B              │     │
│     │   Project to develop programme    │     │
│     │      (Preparation Project)        │     │
│     │  ┌─────────────────────────────┐  │     │
│     │  │          STAGE 1            │  │     │
│     │  │ Information gathering,       │  │     │
│     │  │ consultation and survey     │  │     │
│     │  └─────────────────────────────┘  │     │
│     │  ┌─────────────────────────────┐  │     │
│     │  │          STAGE 2            │  │     │
│     │  │  Assessment and analysis    │  │     │
│     │  └─────────────────────────────┘  │     │
│     │  ┌─────────────────────────────┐  │     │
│     │  │          STAGE 3            │  │     │
│     │  │     Programme design        │  │     │
│     │  └─────────────────────────────┘  │     │
│     └───────────────────────────────────┘     │
│                      ▼                        │
│            ┌─────────────────────┐            │
│            │      STAGE 4        │            │
│            │ Programme           │            │
│            │ implementation      │            │
│            │ and management      │            │
│            └─────────────────────┘            │
│      ┌──────────────┐   ┌──────────────┐      │
│      │   STAGE 5    │   │   STAGE 6    │      │
│      │  Evaluation  │   │  Adjustment  │      │
│      └──────────────┘   └──────────────┘      │
│                                               │
│       The Guidelines in a programme cycle     │
│                                               │
└─────────────────────────────────────────────┘
```

**The Guidelines in a programme cycle**

## Section A: Preparation Phase

Section A covers the steps to establish a project to carry out the exercise of preparing a programme. It is assumed that an instruction has been given by central government to undertake the exercise, so the steps start from there. This preparation project may take about six months to complete, depending on the size and complexity of the programme area.

The output of Section A will be a costed proposal for a project to develop a programme.

## Section B: Project to Develop a Programme (Preparation Project)

### Stage 1: Information gathering, consultation and survey

Information gathering is necessary to understand the whole context of the proposed programme. Although the users may be very familiar with their working situation, it can still be very useful for them to step out of their day-to-day work and take a fresh look at the context. The type of information to gather includes social, economic and health, both quantitative and qualitative, as well as the technical issues of water resources and supply and sanitation.

It is essential that the views of people at all levels are taken into account. This includes the beneficiaries' views of their own problems and needs, and their ideas of possible solutions. The information-gathering process addresses this by looking at each different level — central, provincial or regional, district and village. As far as possible, participatory methods should be used.

### Stage 2: Assessment and analysis

The information gathered is then assessed and analysed before being presented in a **participatory planning workshop**. Representatives from the various different levels and areas of expertise should be involved in this workshop, including representatives from community level. The workshop uses participatory methods such as problem identification and problem tree analysis to set objectives and activities in each of the areas, and SWOT analysis to look at the institutions in the sector. The outputs from the planning workshop are then reviewed by the sector professionals to ensure that all the activities necessary to achieve those objectives have been considered.

### Stage 3: Design

This stage covers the preparation of broad objectives, detailed specific objectives, activities, a budget and a timeframe. The Guidelines help in the outline design of activities but stop at that point. Detailed design is assumed to be part of programme implementation.

The design of the Programme in Stage 3 includes not only the specific components of a water and sanitation programme, but also prepares the systems that will be needed for implementation and management in Stage 4 and evaluation in Stage 5.

### Implementation

The actual running of the programme — Stages 4, 5 and 6 — are not part of these Guidelines and Manual.

## Structure and organisation

As implied by the title, this document is arranged in two parts, the Guidelines and a supporting Manual.

The **Guidelines** (this book) consist of:

- flowcharts outlining the steps in the process; with
- introductions to each of the steps highlighting key points; and
- checklists.

The **Manual** (the accompanying CD):

- explains how to carry out the steps in the Guidelines;
- provides additional information and details;
- provides forms and tables for the user to use for surveys and analysis of information. Most of the forms are hyperlinked to MS Word versions which users can open and edit electronically; and
- refers to other publications for further guidance.

The Guidelines and the Manual are cross-referenced by a decimal numbering system: the basic numbers shown in the flowcharts are prefixed by G in the Guidelines and M in the Manual. These are summarised in Table 1.

The Guidelines and Manual are presented in a number of levels:

Sections: There are two sections: A for Preparation Phase and B for the Project to Develop the Programme.

Stages: Section B is divided into three Stages, based on the first three stages of a standard programme cycle (see Figure 1). These are 1, 2 and 3 in the decimal numbered referencing system.

The stages are divided into the main activities and processes. In the decimal numbered referencing system, these are 1.1, 2.1, 2.2, 2.3, etc.

The activities and processes are further sub-divided into tasks, pieces of information, issues to consider, lists and forms. In the decimal numbered referencing system, these are 2.1.1, 2.1.2, 2.3.1, etc.

### Table 1: Cross-referencing system of the Guidelines and Manual

| | Section A | | | Section B | | |
|---|---|---|---|---|---|---|
| | **Flowchart** | **Guidelines** | **Manual** | **Flowchart** | **Guidelines** | **Manual** |
| **Cross-reference numbering*** | A1 | GA1 | MA1 | 1 | G1 | M1 |
| | A2 | GA2 | MA2 | 2 | G2 | M2 |
| | A3 | GA3 | MA3 | 2.1 | G2.1 | M2.1 |
| | | | | | G2.1.1 | M2.1.1 |
| | Tables and Forms are numbered according to the section and level in which they are located. | | | | | |

\* There is not always a corresponding reference number in the Manual for a number in the Guidelines: e.g. G1.3.3 does not have a corresponding M1.3.3.

## Flowcharts

The flowcharts are like road maps of the process. They show you where you are, where you want to go, and how to get there. Like maps, the flowcharts have various scales. Some present the overview of a whole stage at small scale, others show the steps and sub-steps within a stage at large scale.

The various shapes used in the flowcharts are based on standard flowchart symbols, which have different meanings. The ones used in the Guidelines are:

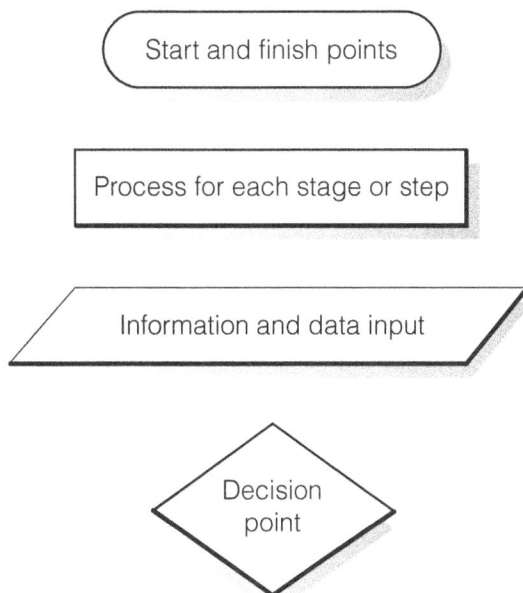

Start and finish points

Process for each stage or step

Information and data input

Decision point

The process boxes are numbered with the cross-reference numbering system so that you can easily go to the description of that stage or step in either the Guidelines or the Manual. For example, in the Flowchart of Stage 2 (in Section G2), 2.3 Planning Workshop refers to G2.3 and M2.3 for summary and detailed descriptions respectively.

## Using the Guidelines and Manual

The Guidelines and Manual are designed to assist a team of government staff to plan and design a programme. They provide the team with support, advice and further information about the various subjects and issues involved in the various stages of information gathering, assessment, analysis and design.

The suggested team should be composed of representatives and specialists of the various ministries and departments involved in the water, sanitation and hygiene promotions sector, from district level up through regional level to central government level as appropriate.

Copies of the Guidelines and Manual should be given to each member of the team. The members of the team should be assigned responsibility for particular steps and sub-steps according to their discipline, specialist knowledge, skills and competence.

The stages and steps in the Guidelines and Manual are intended to be followed in roughly the order presented. In some of the steps, the sub-steps can be done at the same time by the relevant team members. In other steps, the sub-steps should be done sequentially in the order presented. The context shows whether this is necessary. The order of decision-making can be important. In some places, it will be necessary to make a decision on one step before another can be developed.

The Guidelines and Manual allow for a Briefing Workshop (G1.2 and M1.2) to start the Preparation Project. This is to allow the members of the team to get to know each other, to understand the Guidelines and the assignment, and to provide training on the participatory processes, if necessary. It is also suggested that regular meetings of the Core Team and others should be held to plan the work, assign individual tasks and monitor progress. Guidance on these meetings is not provided, as they are considered to be standard management practice.

## Finally

The most important thing to remember when using these Guidelines and Manual is that they are just that — guidelines. They provide suggestions of what is considered necessary for planning in the opinion of the authors. You, the users, are the ones who have to make decisions and be responsible for the results. You should take or leave what is suggested here, as you think appropriate. You may need to include additional information or take special factors into account. You may have a different way of doing things that can be equally good or probably better. You are the ones who understand your own context and how methods may or may not work.

Be open, however, to alternative ways of doing things that may not be familiar to you. Discuss and debate with your team and with other people with an interest in the rural water supply and sanitation sector. In particular, involve the people with the most interest, the communities, householders, women, children and men who will be using the water and sanitation services and resources and who are directly responsible for their health and hygiene.

# Section A:
# Preparation Phase

**A**

**G**

## Objective of Section A

To produce:

a proposal for a project to prepare an integrated water and sanitation sector programme for a specific area, including the resources required for the project, a budget, a timetable and a plan

based on:

an instruction with terms of reference from the government, and consideration of the programme area.

This section provides guidance on the various steps necessary for a small team of government staff to develop a project (the 'Preparation Project') to plan and design a water supply and sanitation sector programme, including hygiene promotion, water resource management and institutional strengthening, for a particular area. It includes:

■ **Terms of Reference** – these may be pre-set by the instructing authority (e.g. a minister or senior government official), or the instructing authority may request draft ToR to be prepared for it to issue. The Guidelines suggest the issues that should be covered by the ToR. Even if the ToR are pre-set, it may be worth considering the range of issues suggested here during the development of the Preparation Project. It may be possible to negotiate changes to the ToR. In any case, use of this step may help to ensure that the Preparation Project has the scope to address the range of issues in the sector.

■ **The planning level** – looks at the important decision concerning which administrative level — central, regional, or possibly district — should be responsible for organising, managing and undertaking the Preparation Project.

■ **The Planning Team** – suggests the types of skills and experience necessary for the Core Team which will undertake the Preparation Project, and the associated ministries and departments that may be involved. It also suggests other people and skills that may be needed for different parts of the preparation project.

■ **Preparation of a timetable** – provides information on the activities and factors to be considered in estimating the time required for the Preparation Project, and a format for developing a Gant chart (bar chart) for this.

■ **Estimating resources** – gives suggestions on the resources required for the Preparation Project (apart from people).

■ **Estimating costs** – provides formats for producing a budget based on the people, other resources and time required.

■ **Proposal for the Preparation Project** – suggests the format and subjects to be covered in the formal submission requesting authorisation and funding to undertake the Preparation Project.

**A1: Instruction from Government to prepare programme with**
**A2: Terms of Reference**

Start
**SECTION A**

A3: Planning level

A4: Ministries to be involved in Programme

A5/A8: Activities in Preparation Project

A6: Staffing of the Preparation Project Team

Are all the skills required available?

No → Terms of Reference and person specification for external consultants

Yes

Refine/revise activities for Preparation Project

Revise Preparation Project

A7: Time-table for Preparation Project

A9: Other resources required

A10: Budget for Preparation Project

A11: Proposal for Preparation Project

Submit Proposal for Preparation Project for approval

Decision from Government to proceed with Preparation Project as proposed

No: revise

No: Cancel → STOP

Yes

**Go to SECTION B Preparation Project**

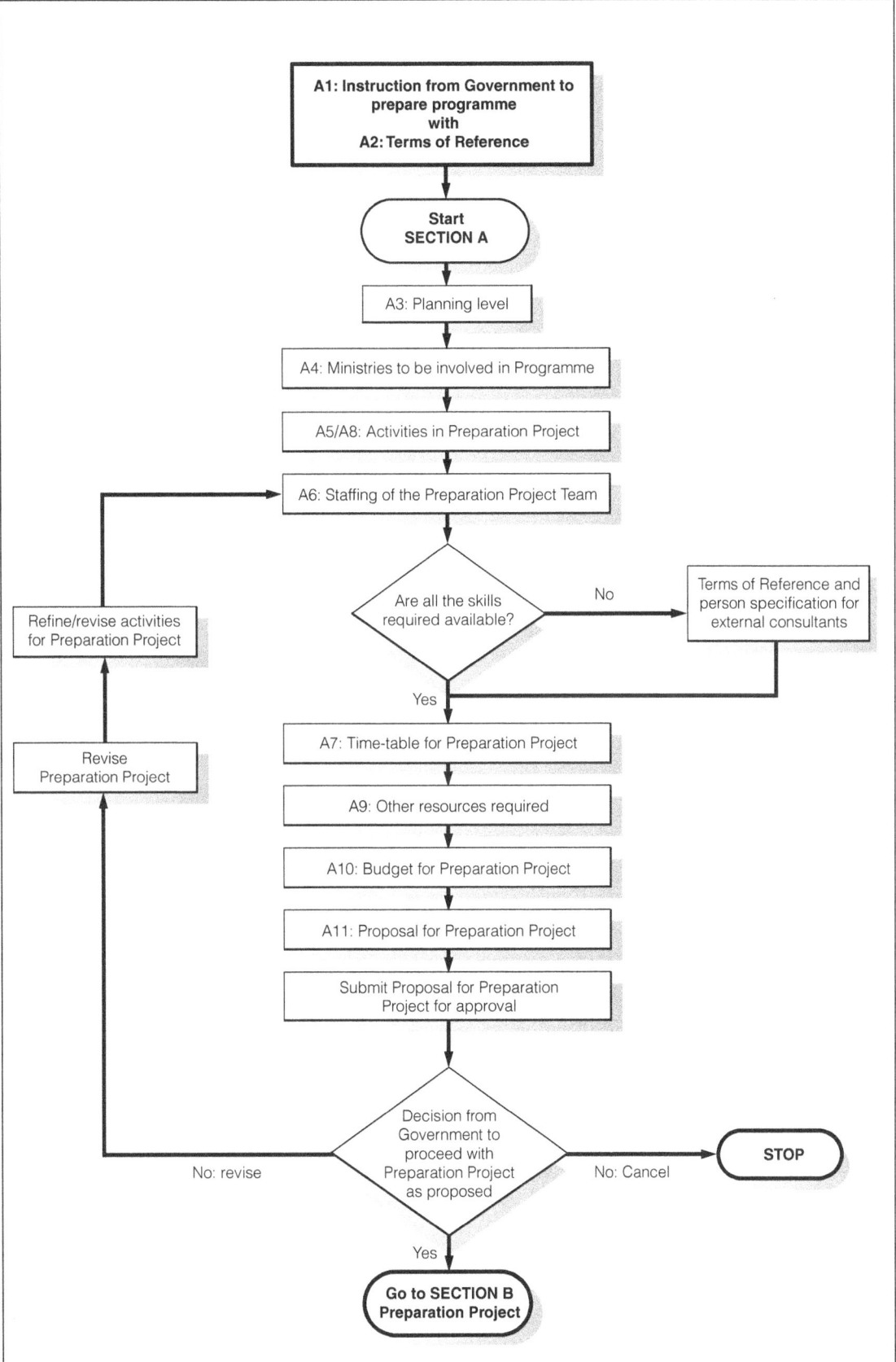

**Flowchart of Section A: Preparation phase**

A

G

# A

G

# Guidelines

## GA1  Instruction to Prepare Programme

The instruction from the government or commissioning ministry should include detailed Terms of Reference to make clear exactly what is required and to guide the Planning Team in its work. The instruction should be something like:

*prepare a project, including a plan and budget, for planning and designing a rural water supply and sanitation sector programme proposal, and submit the project plan and budget for approval before proceeding with the programme planning and design. The programme proposal should include the items listed in the Terms of Reference.*

## GA2  Terms of Reference

Table GA2.1 gives a suggested list of the items that should be specified in the ToR. There may be others depending on the local circumstances.

**Table GA2.1: Items to be specified in the Terms of Reference**

| Item |
|---|
| Geographical area to be covered |
| Groups to be covered:<br>• social groups<br>• ethnic groups<br>• settlement sizes<br>• rural<br>• peri-urban<br>• institutions |
| Programme components:<br>• water supply<br>• water resource management<br>• hygiene promotion<br>• sanitation<br>• community management<br>• institutional strengthening/capacity building |
| Time-scale of programme |
| Department and person responsible |
| Other ministries and departments with responsibilities or involvement in the sector at various administrative levels |
| Implementing agencies:<br>• regional and district government department<br>• NGOs<br>• CBOs<br>• Private sector companies |
| Coverage:<br>• targets for water supply – coverage and operation<br>• targets for sanitation<br>• rehabilitation of water supplies<br>• hygiene promotion |
| Maintenance systems for water supply |
| Arrangements for cost sharing:<br>• capital costs<br>• recurrent operation and maintenance costs |

**A**

**G**

## GA3  Planning level

It is important to make the right decision about which administrative level will be responsible for the Preparation Project for planning and designing the programme. The administrative level is the level at which the Core Team is managed and to which it is responsible. Should the Preparation Project be organised and managed centrally or regionally?

This is probably one of the first decisions that will have to be made, but it needs careful consideration because it is likely to have far-reaching consequences. It may even affect the subsequent success or failure of the programme.

Usually there are two possible levels, central or regional. In some places, a third possible level to consider may be the district. A combination of these levels is also possible, and may represent the best way to benefit from the advantages of each. The advantages and disadvantages of each level are shown in Table GA3.1.

**Table GA3.1: Advantages and disadvantages of different administrative levels**

| Level | Advantages | Disadvantages |
|---|---|---|
| Central | <ul><li>specialist skills and knowledge may be readily available</li><li>staff are likely to have access to offices, information and data at central level</li></ul> | <ul><li>may be out of touch with problems and issues in the programme area</li></ul> |
| Regional | <ul><li>promotes a sense of ownership of the programme by the people who will be implementing it</li><li>should know of the problems and issues in the programme area</li></ul> | <ul><li>may lack authority for planning programme</li></ul> |
| District | <ul><li>detailed knowledge of the area</li></ul> | <ul><li>may lack authority for planning programme</li><li>may lack the skills and experience necessary for programme planning and design</li></ul> |

The methodology proposed in these Guidelines is for staff from all the levels to work together. A Core Team of staff with appropriate skills and experience from the various levels can be assembled to implement the Preparation Project (MA6). The skills and experience of this team may need to be supplemented by the use of consultants.

**A**

**G**

## GA4  Ministries to be involved in programme

A number of different ministries and departments may be involved in the sector, either directly with explicit responsibilities, or indirectly where they are carrying out a particular role.  The ministries could include:

- Planning
- Water resources
- Finance
- Local government
- Women's affairs
- Rural development
- Agriculture
- Power and energy
- Public works
- Health
- Education

The various possible roles and activities are given in the Manual (MA4), with suggestions as to which ministry or department may be undertaking them. It is important to identify all those involved in the sector to see how they can contribute to the planning and design of the programme.

**A**

**G**

## GA5　Stages and steps in Preparation Project

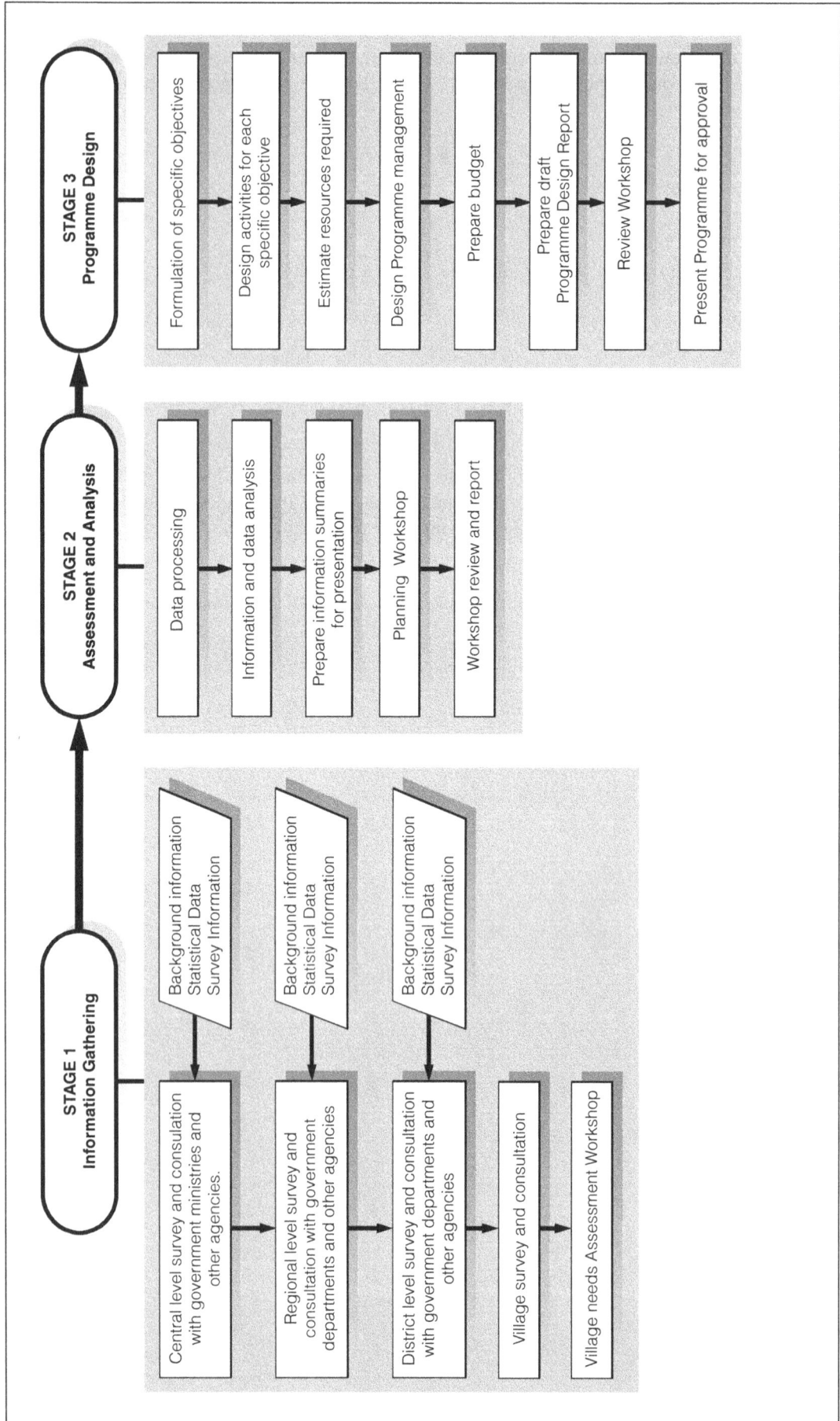

**STAGE 1**
**Information Gathering**

Central level survey and consultation with government ministries and other agencies.

Regional level survey and consultation with government departments and other agencies

District level survey and consultation with government departments and other agencies

Village survey and consultation

Village needs Assessment Workshop

Background information
Statistical Data
Survey Information

Background information
Statistical Data
Survey Information

Background information
Statistical Data
Survey Information

**STAGE 2**
**Assessment and Analysis**

Data processing

Information and data analysis

Prepare information summaries for presentation

Planning Workshop

Workshop review and report

**STAGE 3**
**Programme Design**

Formulation of specific objectives

Design activities for each specific objective

Estimate resources required

Design Programme management

Prepare budget

Prepare draft Programme Design Report

Review Workshop

Present Programme for approval

## GA6 Staffing of the Preparation Project team

To carry out the programme Preparation Project, it is necessary to form a Planning Team. This team should be formed at the level appropriate to the programme, i.e. it may be at central, regional or district level. A special consideration is:

■ Do the necessary skills and expertise exist at the level chosen, or will it be necessary to bring expertise in from a different level?

It may also be necessary to have people of the same professional discipline from more than one level. For example, a planner working at central level may have a very different perspective than a planner working at regional or district level, so it may be worth having planners from both levels on the team.

As far as possible the team should consist of people who will be implementing and managing the operation stage of the programme. The Manual suggests people who should be considered to participate in the planning and design of the programme (MA6). Three degrees of participation are possible:

■ member of the Core Team, leading and responsible for the Preparation Project;
■ co-opted for specific assignments during the Preparation Project where additional skills are required (e.g. specialised government staff, consultants, staff from other organisations such as NGOs); and
■ consulted during the process of the preparation project.

A

G

A

G

## GA7  Estimating time

The time needed for most activities will depend on the resources — especially people — that are available. Some activities will need a certain period of time irrespective of the number of people, e.g. the planning workshop. Others will depend on various factors. In particular, the time needed for the village-level consultations and surveys will vary according to the number of villages that should be surveyed to be representative of the area. If the area is more complex socially, ethnically or geographically then more villages will have to be covered.

The factors to consider for estimating the time needed for each activity are given in Table MA7.1 in the Manual (MA7).

### GA7.1  Preparation of timetable

To be able to plan, budget for and monitor the project it is necessary to prepare a timetable. This is best done in the form of a bar chart or Gant chart. A form for this, with the activities listed, is given in the Manual (Form MA7.1).

## GA8  Planning activities for Preparation Project: Summary

The Manual (MA8) provides forms for summarising the detailed planning of the various activities. This summary should help in estimating the budget needed for the Preparation Project. The outline of the various activities is given in Flowchart GA5, and fuller explanations are in the Manual.

**A**

**G**

## GA9  Estimating other resources

The various items needed to support the Project need to be allowed for and costed. The following lists suggest the items likely to be needed. Some items will be needed for the whole period, others for part of the period.

It may be possible to 'borrow' some things without cost from government departments, but others may have to be paid for. Estimating forms are given in the Manual (MA9 and MA11).

### Office space

It is advisable to have an office especially for the Project Preparation. This will help the team to concentrate and should help in team-building if it is separate from the members' normal workplaces.

The area should be large enough to accommodate the team members, the administrative support staff, additional temporary team members and the storage of documents and information.

A venue for the Planning Workshop, with accommodation for up to 50 people, will also be necessary.

### Transport

This will be needed for:

■ information gathering at all levels
■ surveys and consultation at central level
■ surveys and consultation at regional level
■ surveys and consultation at district level
■ village level survey and consultation

### Administrative support

■ office administrator
■ secretary
■ computer operator
■ driver
■ caretaker
■ etc.

### Office equipment, consumables and running costs

■ furniture
■ computers
■ printers
■ photocopier
■ telephones
■ filing cabinets
■ office rent
■ electricity and telephone charges
■ paper
■ etc.

A

G

## GA10 Estimating costs

To prepare a budget for the Preparation Project, you will have to estimate the costs of each of the activities in terms of:

- staff salaries and costs
- transport and travel allowances
- equipment and other resources
- fees for maps, searches, etc.

To assist with this process, example forms (Forms MA10 and MA10.1) giving a method for building up the costs are provided for each of these headings in the Manual (MA10). Your government may have its own procedure for estimating costs, so you should decide whether to follow your government system or to use these estimating sheets.

The objective is to show clearly how costs are estimated, and the costs of each part of the Preparation Project. This should make them easier to justify if there are any questions about the cost of the Preparation Project, or if there is any change to the Project.

## GA11 Proposal for Preparation Project

In order to get approval to proceed with the Preparation Project, it will probably be necessary to submit a proposal, based on the Terms of Reference, explaining the Project and its methodology, plan and cost.

The proposal should show how each of the items in the Terms of Reference will be addressed, adding detail and information, particularly if any variation from the ToR has been found necessary. Thus the proposal should include:

**A**

**G**

### Table GA11.1: Things to be covered in the proposal

| Item in ToR | Proposal | Variations from ToR |
|---|---|---|
| Geographical area to be covered | Confirm with description (and map) | any additional or reduced area, with justification |
| Target user groups to be covered:<br>• social groups<br>• ethnic groups<br>• settlement sizes | Confirm with description | any additional groups, or groups to be excluded, with justification |
| Programme components:<br>• water supply<br>• water management<br>• hygiene education<br>• sanitation<br>• institutional strengthening | Confirm with description | any additional components, or components to be excluded or only partially covered, with justification |
| Department responsible | Confirm | |
| Other ministries and departments with responsibilities or involvement in the sector | Confirm ministries and departments | any other departments that should be included, or any specified in the ToR that are not willing to take part in the Preparation Project |
| Implementing agencies | Confirm implementing agencies | any others that should be included, or any specified in the ToR that are not willing to take part in the Preparation Project |
| Coverage:<br>• targets for water supply<br>• targets for sanitation<br>• rehabilitation of water supplies<br>• hygiene promotion | Confirm | note any proposed changes, with reasons |
| Maintenance systems for water supply | Confirm | note any proposed changes, with reasons |
| Arrangements for cost sharing:<br>• capital costs<br>• recurrent maintenance costs | Confirm | note any proposed changes, with reasons |
| | Methodology for Preparation Project | |
| | Activities | |
| | Time-scale for Preparation Project, including bar chart | |
| | Staffing and resources required | |
| | Budget | |

**A**

G

# Section B:
# Project to develop programme

# Guidelines

B

# B

# Stage 1:
# Information gathering, consultations and surveys

B

G1

## Objective of Stage 1

To gather information and understand the issues, challenges and problems in the water supply and sanitation sector in the programme area from the viewpoint of both government staff at various levels and communities themselves, so that the planning is based on the real context of the area.

## Introduction

Information gathering is necessary to understand the whole context of the proposed programme. The members of the Planning Team may be very familiar with their working situations, but it can still be very useful for them to step out of the day-to-day work and take a fresh look at the context. Information needs to be gathered on social, economic and health issues, as well as the technical aspects of water resources and supply and sanitation.

It is essential that views at all levels are taken into account. This includes the beneficiaries' views of their own problems and needs. The information-gathering process addresses this by looking at each different level — central, provincial or regional, and district — and by carrying out sample surveys in villages. Background information and statistical data should also be collected at each level. As far as possible, participatory methods should be used. The village surveys are consolidated in Village Needs Assessment Workshops with village representatives in each district.

As shown in the **Flowchart of Stage 1**, Stage 1 starts with a **Briefing Workshop** for the Planning Team. This has two parts. The first is an introduction to the Guidelines and Manual and the proposed planning process. The second part is for training on the methods and techniques to be used. For some members of the Team, this should be a useful refresher in participatory methods, for others it may be an introduction to the techniques. Overall, it should build confidence in the Team so that they are better able to undertake consultations and surveys.

The **Consultation and surveys** cover the three levels of government administration, central, regional or provincial, and district, with **Statistical data** and **Background information** being collected at each level.

For the **Village surveys and consultations** the Team should work together with appropriate staff from the district administration who may be more familiar with village work. Then the village surveys are consolidated for each district by holding a **Village Needs Assessment Workshop** with representatives from each of the communities visited in the district. This is the villagers' chance to analyse their own situation and to define their needs and expectation of the programme, which is intended to be for them.

### Definitions

| | |
|---|---|
| Background information: | information about the context in which the water supply and sanitation sector works |
| Statistical data: | statistics from official reports and other documents |
| Survey: | systematic collection of information |
| Consultation: | meetings and discussions with people to understand the issues and problems in the sector |

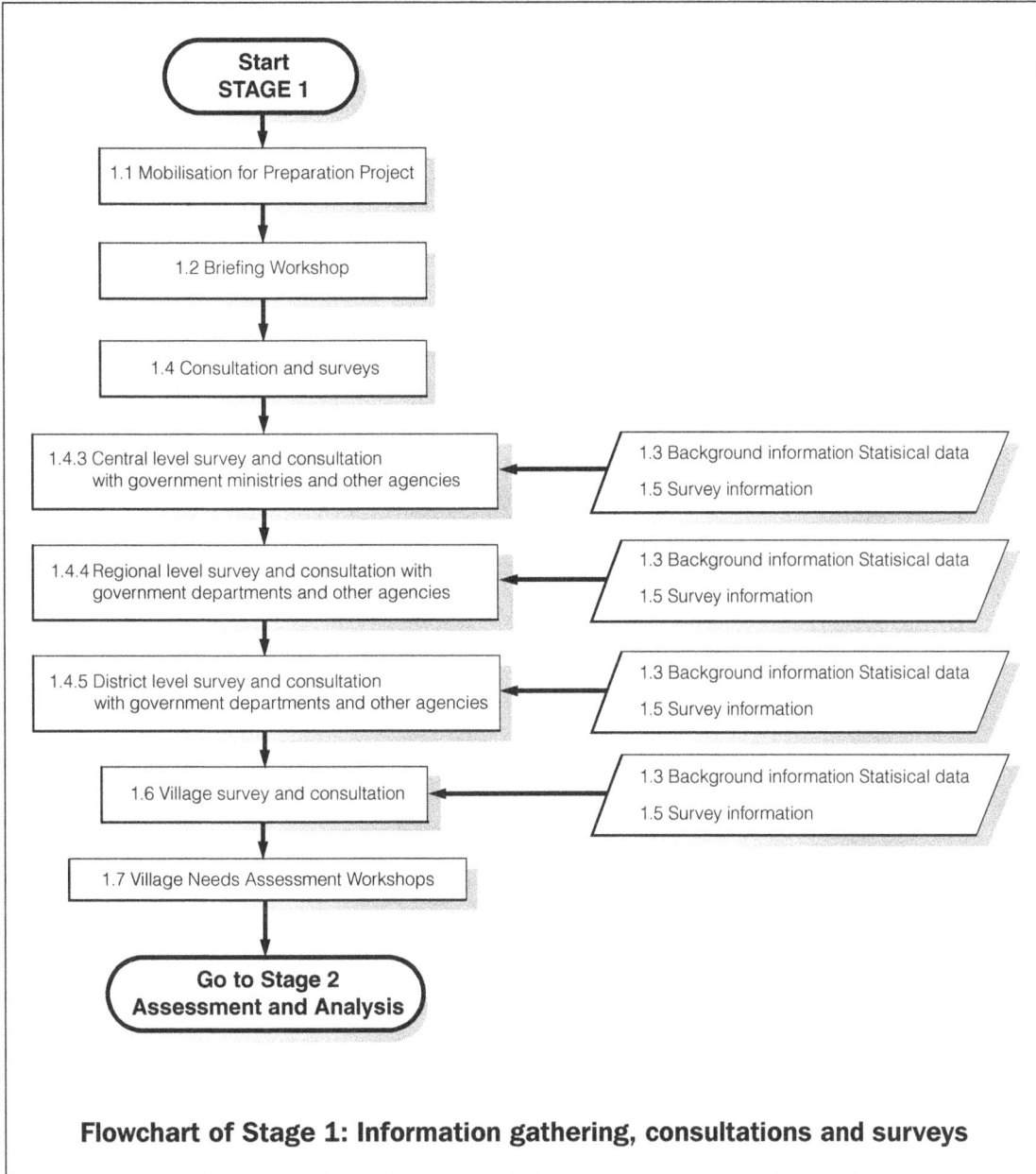

```
                    ┌──────────────────┐
                    │      Start       │
                    │     STAGE 1      │
                    └──────────────────┘
                             │
                             ▼
         ┌──────────────────────────────────────┐
         │ 1.1 Mobilisation for Preparation Project │
         └──────────────────────────────────────┘
                             │
                             ▼
         ┌──────────────────────────────────────┐
         │        1.2 Briefing Workshop         │
         └──────────────────────────────────────┘
                             │
                             ▼
         ┌──────────────────────────────────────┐
         │      1.4 Consultation and surveys    │
         └──────────────────────────────────────┘
                             │
                             ▼
  ┌────────────────────────────────────────────┐      ┌──────────────────────────────────────────┐
  │ 1.4.3 Central level survey and consultation │ ◄─── │ 1.3 Background information Statisical data │
  │  with government ministries and other agencies │    │ 1.5 Survey information                     │
  └────────────────────────────────────────────┘      └──────────────────────────────────────────┘
                             │
                             ▼
  ┌────────────────────────────────────────────┐      ┌──────────────────────────────────────────┐
  │ 1.4.4 Regional level survey and consultation with │◄─│ 1.3 Background information Statisical data │
  │  government departments and other agencies  │      │ 1.5 Survey information                     │
  └────────────────────────────────────────────┘      └──────────────────────────────────────────┘
                             │
                             ▼
  ┌────────────────────────────────────────────┐      ┌──────────────────────────────────────────┐
  │ 1.4.5 District level survey and consultation│ ◄─── │ 1.3 Background information Statisical data │
  │  with government departments and other agencies │  │ 1.5 Survey information                     │
  └────────────────────────────────────────────┘      └──────────────────────────────────────────┘
                             │
                             ▼
     ┌──────────────────────────────────────┐          ┌──────────────────────────────────────────┐
     │ 1.6 Village survey and consultation   │ ◄─────── │ 1.3 Background information Statisical data │
     └──────────────────────────────────────┘          │ 1.5 Survey information                     │
                             │                          └──────────────────────────────────────────┘
                             ▼
     ┌──────────────────────────────────────┐
     │ 1.7 Village Needs Assessment Workshops │
     └──────────────────────────────────────┘
                             │
                             ▼
                  ┌──────────────────────┐
                  │   Go to Stage 2      │
                  │ Assessment and Analysis │
                  └──────────────────────┘
```

**Flowchart of Stage 1: Information gathering, consultations and surveys**

B

G1

**B**

**G1**

**Information gathering,
consultations and surveys**

## G1.1 Mobilisation for Preparation Project

### Formation of Planning Team

The Preparation Phase in Section A describes the points to consider and the type of people required for a Planning Team (GA3, MA4 and MA6). The actual people now have to be selected and appointed, and/or seconded from other ministries and department.

To ensure a cohesive and effective Team, it is important to select staff with the appropriate seniority and experience. The Team should be compatible in terms of government grading. Based on the pilot study in Zambia, the grading of a Team Leader as a professional manager with 15 years of experience or more would be appropriate. The other members of the Team should be from a similar or lower grade for a technical specialist. It is important not to appoint people who are too senior. They are likely to have many other calls on their time, so may not be able to concentrate full-time on the Preparation Project. Tensions between Team members may be caused if specialists have a much higher grading than the Team Leader. All Team members should have substantial experience in their professional field, probably not less than 10 years.

The appointment of suitable administrative support staff will also have to be arranged.

### Consultants

One of the original concepts behind the Guidelines was that governments should be able to design their own programmes without the need for external consultants. The experience from the pilot study in Zambia shows that this may be too optimistic. The Zambian team clearly had the ability to plan and design a programme — what they lacked was the experience and confidence. Consultants may still be needed, but their role should very different to the traditional one of leading and managing the process. Consultants should be used in a technical advisory capacity, supporting and advising the national Team and providing training where required. Management and control of the process should be the responsibility of the national Team.

Defining the need for consultancy services, writing terms of reference, and selecting and appointing consultants requires special care and attention. The development banks and other organisations may be able to provide guidance on this. The Asian Development Bank has published *Guidelines on the Use of Consultants by Asian Development Bank and its Borrowers*. The International Labour Office has another useful book, *How to select and use consultants: A client's guide* (1993).

### Office facilities, equipment and transport

The office accommodation, equipment, transport, etc., as described in Section A (GA9) will have to be arranged in time for the Team to start work.

**B**

**G1**

**B**

**G1**

**Information gathering,
consultations and surveys**

## G1.2 Briefing Workshop

Making a good start to the Preparation Project is obviously essential, because it will influence how the rest of the relatively short project will proceed and succeed. It is also important to have a clear start to the project. To help with this, it is recommended that a Briefing Workshop be held for the Core Planning Team and other people who will join the Team for parts of the process. The objectives for this workshop are:

- to enable the Planning Team to get to know each other and start team building;
- to enable the Planning Team to understand the Guidelines and the assignment;
- to help the Planning Team understand the approaches to be used, which may be different to their normal procedures;
- to promote a common understanding of and commitment to the process; and
- to refresh the Team's participatory assessment skills.

This meeting may need to last for three days, including training in participatory methodologies. Full session plans for the Briefing Workshop are given in the Manual (M1.2).

**B**

**G1**

**B**

**G1**

Information gathering,
consultations and surveys

## G1.3  Background information and statistical data

### G1.3.1 Maps of the programme area

Various types of map will be useful for setting the context for planning and programme design and for understanding aspects of the programme areas. Table G1.3.1 gives a checklist of possible types of map.

**Table G1.3.1: Types of map**

| Type of map | Check |
|---|:---:|
| Topographic | ☐ |
| Administrative boundaries | ☐ |
| Roads | ☐ |
| Geological | ☐ |
| Hydrogeological | ☐ |
| Rainfall | ☐ |
| Settlement patterns | ☐ |
| Population density | ☐ |
| Land use | ☐ |
| Aerial photographs | ☐ |
| Satellite imagery | ☐ |

More detail on maps is provided in the Manual (M1.3.1).

**B**

**G1**

### G1.3.2 Institutional arrangements

Information on the institutional arrangements should be collected during the consultations and surveys at each level.

#### *Organisations*

It is important to identify all the organisations working in and/or contributing to the sector. These may be broadly classified as follows:

- government
- donor
- international organisations and NGOs (operational)
- local NGOs
- private sector

Table M1.3.2, in the Manual (M1.3.2), can be used to compile a list of relevant organisations and show their areas of responsibility or skills. During the consultations and surveys organisations can be added to the table as they are identified.

#### *Co-ordination, policy-making and regulation/control*

The present responsibility for co-ordination in the sector should be defined and the mechanism recorded. An assessment of whether the system is working will form part of the survey and consultation at the different levels.

Roles and responsibilities in policy-making and regulation and control should be defined. Table M1.3.2 can be used to list these.

#### *Types of implementation and activities*

The different specialist areas of implementation and activities should be identified, by organisation. This will help to show up areas where there is limited capacity or coverage, and any complete gaps in coverage. Table M1.3.2 should help in this process.

### G1.3.3 Government legislation, policies and plans

Copies of any legislation and policies relevant to the sector should be obtained, including copies of drafts if in process. Table G1.3.3a suggests some of the possibilities.

**Table G1.3.3a: Legislation and policies relevant to the sector**

|  | Check |
|---|---|
| water resources | ☐ |
| rural water supply | ☐ |
| sanitation | ☐ |
| health | ☐ |
| gender | ☐ |
| rural development | ☐ |
| NGOs | ☐ |
| agricultural water use | ☐ |
| industrial water use | ☐ |
|  | ☐ |
|  | ☐ |

Similarly, copies of government plans and donors' plans should be obtained and any parts dealing with the above areas highlighted. Table 1.3.3b shows relevant types of plans.

**Table G1.3.3b: Plans relevant to the programme**

|  | Check |
|---|---|
| Five-year plans (or other planning period) | ☐ |
| rolling plans | ☐ |
| sector plans and reviews | ☐ |
| donors' plans | ☐ |
| NGOs' plans | ☐ |
|  | ☐ |
|  | ☐ |

**B**

**G1**

### G1.3.4 Population

Population growth rates are needed to estimate the number of people to be served in the future, in accordance with the time horizon for the programme.

More detailed information on aspects such as:

- urban and rural populations;
- populations in each district or sub-division of the area;
- settlement patterns;
- populations densities; and
- migration, etc.

will help to refine the programme design and enable particular groups to be identified and targeted.

**Wherever possible, this statistical data should be dis-aggregated by gender and age**, that is, the figures for men, for women and for children should be given separately, as well as the totals. This is to analyse whether women's needs and men's needs and contexts are the same or different. Dis-aggregated statistics can also be used for monitoring to ensure that different gender needs are being met.

There may be various sources for such data, at the different administrative levels — central, regional and district. An important document would be the most recent census from the government statistics office. The following list suggests this and other possible sources:

- census
- other government documents
- statistics office
- other government departments
- local knowledge
- surveys
- other programmes and project data

More detail on population data is provided in the Manual (M1.3.4).

B

G1

### G1.3.5 Socio-economic information

People are the reason for any development programme or project. Thus it is essential to understand the social, cultural and economic characteristics of the people in the programme area in order to develop a programme that fits their needs, aspirations and circumstances. This understanding must include the dynamics of gender — the roles of women and men, girls and boys, and the relationships between them. If these are ignored or not understood, the prospects for the success of the programme may be adversely affected.

More detailed information on aspects such as:

- ethnic and religious sub-groups;
- occupations of people;
- sources of income;
- assets and income;
- types of economic systems;
- literacy rates;
- women-headed households; and
- disabled people; etc.

**Again, wherever possible, this information should be dis-aggregated by gender and age.** There may be various sources for such data, at the different administrative levels — central, regional and district. An important document would be the most recent census from the government statistics office. The following list suggests this and other possible sources:

- census
- other government documents
- statistics office
- other government departments
- local knowledge
- surveys
- other programmes and project data

More detail on socio-economic data is provided in the Manual (M1.3.5).

B

G1

### G1.3.6 Water resources

All water supply programmes require a proper understanding of all the available resources, their quantity and sustainability, quality, and the location and accessibility of water resources. There are three broad areas of enquiry:

- **Climate**:      rainfall, evaporation, trends, major zones

- **Geography**:   topography, drainage basins, geomorphological zones, land use and soils

- **Geology**:     rock type, rock distribution, nature and depth of weathered zone, and the degree of aquifer confinement

Much of the data for the programme area is likely to be available at central level sufficient to make a broad assessment of the water resource potential. The form of the data may vary but typically could include that shown in Table G1.3.6.

### Table G1.3.6:  Water resources data

| Form of data | Comments |
|---|---|
| Rainfall distribution map | scales from 1:50 000 down to 1:500 000. |
| Evaporation records | from climate data collected at meteorological stations or from evaporation pans |
| Distribution of evaporation | zoned ranges of evaporation, regionally and according to elevation. May need to extrapolate for programme area. |
| Long-term rainfall records | monthly rainfall returns for some stations, perhaps up to 25-year record. May need to extrapolate for programme area. |
| River and stream water-level and flow records | either from fixed flow gauging stations or from current meter gaugings at other sites |
| Surface water flow hydrographs | |
| Inventories of hand-dug wells and drilled wells | Rural water supply programmes may hold inventories of waterpoints. Drilling records and borehole logs may be kept centrally by the appropriate department. |
| Topographical maps | at scales between 1:50 000 and 1:500 000, with streams, rivers, and lakes and catchment divides |
| Geomorphology | can be derived for the programme but may exist as national or provincial syntheses |
| Land use and soil distribution maps | may be available for some areas, perhaps not all. Aerial photographs or satellite images enable a rapid assessment to be made of land use. Soil type may be derived from the geological map if otherwise not available. |
| Geological maps | at a scale of 1:50 000 and less are available for many areas. These portray the type and distribution of particular rock types. Information on weathering and the availability of confined water-bearing strata not apparent from the maps may only be forthcoming from earlier project reports and studies. These data may not be fully available at the beginning of the water resources assessment. |

The process of bringing the data together, identifying shortfalls in the data holdings, and providing a meaningful assessment of the water resources potential of the programme area are described in a series of assessment analyses in the Manual (M2.2.5).

More detail about understanding and assessing water resources is provided in the Manual (M1.3.6).

### G1.3.7  Water supply and waste disposal

A major part of this data-gathering and assessment exercise is to find out what water supply and waste disposal facilities already exist in the programme area. Data gathering falls broadly into three areas:

- water supply coverage
- water usage
  - domestic
  - agricultural
  - urban
  - industrial
  - recreation
- latrine coverage
- latrine usage
- solid waste disposal facilities
- pollution from waste disposal

This should provide a number of pieces of basic information:

- existing coverage with improved water facilities
- use of traditional water sources
- existing patterns and trends
- existing coverage with improved sanitation facilities
- traditional methods for disposal of excreta
- information on existing technical choices
- yield and quantity of water facilities
- particular problems and problem areas

These data can then be used for the hydrogeological and hydrological assessments (M2.2.5) and to provide additional information regarding existing use of the available water resource and the stress placed on the resource from waste disposal.

Much of the data required to carry out the water supply and waste disposal assessments are likely to be available at government and project level. In this case, however, the programme will need to validate the existing situation during the village consultations and surveys. These surveys should identify failures of waterpoints, disuse of waterpoints in favour of traditional sources, and identify problems (mechanical, hydrogeological, institutional or other) that have occurred with waterpoints. These data are fundamental to the programme design and enable the planners to draw on past experience.

More detail on water supply and sanitation coverage and targets is provided in the Manual (M1.3.7).

**B**

**G1**

### G1.3.8 Hygiene promotion

Hygiene promotion is a process which aims to promote the conditions, attitudes and practices that help to prevent water- and sanitation-related diseases. It is an important component of water supply and sanitation programmes for two reasons: to maximise the potential benefits of improved water supply and sanitation facilities, and to help users to appreciate the need for their proper operation and maintenance to create willingness to contribute to their costs (Boot, 1991). Hygiene education is a part of hygiene promotion.

To prevent water- and sanitation-related diseases and to improve living conditions, facilities have to be used, continuously, by everybody and in a safe way. This requires an interest from both communities and officials. Integrating hygiene promotion with other aspects of water supply and sanitation programmes requires skilful planning and management (*ibid.*). The starting point for this planning is to understand what is currently being done, and what priority is given to hygiene promotion.

Information is needed on a number of different aspects of hygiene promotion, as shown in Table G1.3.8. Detailed questions to obtain this information and forms for compiling it are given in the Manual (M1.3.8, M1.3.9).

### Table G1.3.8: Aspects of hygiene promotion

| Aspect | Detail |
|---|---|
| Funding | <ul><li>government departments and organisations providing funding for hygiene promotion</li><li>budget allocations</li><li>clarity of budget lines</li></ul> |
| Organisations | <ul><li>place of hygiene promotion in organisation of water and sanitation sector</li><li>organisations implementing hygiene promotion</li><li>other organisations undertaking or supporting aspects of hygiene promotion</li><li>collaboration and co-ordination amongst government departments, donors and NGOs in hygiene promotion</li><li>the role of schools in hygiene education and promotion</li></ul> |
| Implementing capacity | <ul><li>human resources for implementation</li><li>supporting resources</li></ul> |
| Health services and facilities | <ul><li>planned and actual health care service provision</li></ul> |
| Health statistics | <ul><li>top ten diseases (morbidity) for adults and children</li><li>incidence of water- and sanitation-related diseases</li><li>infant mortality rate</li></ul> |
| Health policy and planning | <ul><li>health policies of the various organisations</li><li>health plans of the various organisations</li><li>health planning procedures of the various organisations</li><li>international initiatives on hygiene promotion</li></ul> |

### G1.3.9 Health statistics

It is important to collect data on the incidence of the most common diseases (morbidity) to see whether these include water- and sanitation-related diseases. This is needed for advocacy and to justify the water and sanitation programme and the place of hygiene promotion within it.

The diseases and the ranking of their occurrence may be different at the national, regional and district levels. It is important to remember that health statistics are usually based on cases that are referred to the health care systems (at village health posts, clinics and hospitals). The many cases where people are ill but do not get treatment or go to traditional healers are unlikely to be included. Thus, the official statistics may grossly under-represent the true incidence of infectious diseases. Official and unofficial statistics should, therefore, be collected at each level.

A classification system based on transmission routes of infectious water- and sanitation-related diseases has been developed (Cairncross and Feachem, 1993). This is very useful because it helps to show where interventions can be made to reduce the incidence of these diseases. Form M1.3.9 is structured using this classification system. The infant mortality rate (IMR) (0 to 1-year-old) is a sensitive barometer to assess the health of a population. It can differ by area and circumstances, so it can be used to compare the health of different populations in, for example, different geographical areas or different population groups. It is also very important to understand the occurrence of diseases caused by the chemical quality of groundwater, especially arsenic and fluoride.

Form M1.3.9 in the Manual (M1.3.9) can be used to compile the statistics from the various organisations and sources during the consultations and surveys. Possible sources of health statistics are listed in the manual.

**B**

**G1**

### G1.3.10  Funding

As part of the consultation and survey at the different levels, data should be gathered on the funds allocated to the sector by each organisation. This should include both past expenditure and future budgeted or planned spending. To enable a complete picture to be made of the past expenditure, it is probably best to collect the information for the last complete year, with the same year for each organisation. When gathering information from donors and implementers, care should be taken to ensure that funding is not double-counted.

Form M1.3.10 in the Manual (M1.3.10) is provided for collecting funding information from each organisation.

**B**

**G1**

## G1.4   Consultations and surveys – central, regional and district

### G1.4.1 Interviewing

Virtually all the consultations are based on the Team interviewing officials and staff of government departments and organisations. Some of these people may be very senior, others may be much more junior than the person doing the interviewing. Interviewing successfully, which means obtaining the information that is wanted, is a skill that may come naturally to some people, but needs developing in others. The Manual (M1.4.1) provides some points to help in developing these skills. Practice in interviewing is provided as part of the Briefing Workshop (M1.2, Session 6).

**B**

**G1**

## G1.4.2 Central-level consultation and survey

The purpose of the consultation and survey exercise at central level is to understand the policies, views and practices, and the strengths and weaknesses of the government departments and other organisations that will manage, implement and be involved in the programme. This knowledge will be analysed in the Planning Workshop so that objectives and activities can be planned to strengthen the organisations for their roles.

The various organisations should already have been identified as part of the background information collection (G1.3.2 and M1.3.2). The list will probably include the organisations shown in Table G1.4.2.

The consultation on views and practices should include the following:

- sector policies
  - understanding
  - application and practice
- organisation's roles and responsibilities
- organisation's activities
  - plans
  - programmes
  - projects
  - processes
- organisation's future plans and developments
- capability of organisation
- capacity of organisation
- funding
- co-ordination
- perceived issues, challenges, constraints and problems in the sector and facing the organisation

These are described more fully in the Manual (M1.4.2) with suggestions for basic questions to start discussions.

Subject-specific information (e.g. water resources, hygiene education) is covered separately as part of Background information (M1.3) and Survey information (M1.5).
Background information and data, as described previously, should also be collected from each organisation as appropriate.

## Table G1.4.2: Organisations at central level

| government ministries and departments | Water Resources<br>Health<br>Rural Development<br>Planning<br>Public Works<br>Agriculture<br>Education |
|---|---|
| donors: multilateral | World Bank<br>Asian Development Bank<br>African Development Bank<br>European Union<br>etc. |
| donors: bilateral | SIDA<br>DANIDA<br>DFID<br>GTZ<br>USAID<br>FINNIDA<br>NORAD<br>CIDA<br>JICA<br>etc. |
| international organisations and NGOs (operational) | UNICEF<br>UNDP<br>World Health Organisation<br>WaterAid<br>Plan International<br>ActionAid<br>Oxfam<br>CARE<br>etc. |
| local NGOs | |
| private sector | national drilling companies<br>consultants<br>contractors<br>manufacturers<br>resource centres<br>training organisations |

**B**

**G1**

**B**

**G1**

### G1.4.3 Regional-level consultation and survey

The purpose of the consultation and survey exercise at regional level is to understand the policies, views and practices, and the strengths and weaknesses of the government departments and other organisations that will manage, implement and be involved in the programme. This knowledge will be analysed in the Planning Workshop so that objectives and activities can be planned to strengthen the organisations for their roles.

The various organisations should already have been identified as part of the background information collection (G1.3.2 and M1.3.2). The list of organisations to consult will probably include some of those shown in Table G1.4.4.

The consultation on the views and practices of the organisations should include the following:

- sector policies
  - understanding
  - application and practice
- organisation's roles and responsibilities
- organisation's activities
  - plans
  - programmes
  - projects
  - processes
- organisation's future plans and developments
- capability of organisation
- capacity of organisation
- funding
- co-ordination
- perceived issues, challenges, constraints and problems in the sector and facing the organisation

These are described more fully in the Manual (M1.4.3) with suggestions for basic questions to start discussions. Subject-specific information (e.g. water resources, health education, O&M) is covered separately (M1.3 and M1.5).

Background information and data, as described previously, should also be collected from each organisation as appropriate.

**Table G1.4.3: Organisations at regional level**

| government departments | regional government | planning |
| | water resources | public works |
| | health | agriculture |
| | rural development | education |
| international organisations and NGOs (operational) | UNICEF | ActionAid |
| | WHO | Oxfam |
| | WaterAid | CARE |
| | Plan International | etc. |
| local NGOs | Community-based organisations (CBOs) | |
| private sector | drilling companies | |
| | contractors | |

### G1.4.4  District-level consultation and surveys

The purpose of the consultation and surveys at this level is similar to that at regional level, i.e. to obtain the views and practices of the organisations and agencies involved in the sector. See G1.4.3 for the overview and the Manual (M1.4.4, M1.3 and M1.5) for details.

There is, however likely to be a crucial difference in approach at this level, particularly if members of the Core Team are from central level. The intention at district level is not to find out what the formal policies and procedures are, it is to discover the district staff's own understanding and interpretation of these policies. They are the ones who are actually implementing them. They are the ones who are best placed to understand the problems and difficulties of applying the policies.

The interviews with district staff may be especially sensitive if members of the Core Team are associated with making policy at central level. The district staff may be reluctant to discuss the practical realities and problems if they are seen to be criticising policies made by the interviewers. It may also generate a reaction of defensiveness in the interviewers, leading to denial of facts. It is important to establish confidence and trust so that a frank, open expression of views is possible. A demonstrable willingness to learn by the interviewers will help in this. If it works, the results can provide a valuable lesson for everyone.

**B**

**G1**

**B**

**G1**

## G1.5  Survey information gathering

### G1.5.1  Water resources and uses

Knowledge of how water from the various resources is allocated for different uses is important for later assessment of the demand on each resource.  It is also important to understand if there is any conflicting demands for the water between the different uses and users, and whether there are any water rights issues in the area.

Form M1.5.1 in the Manual (M1.5.1) can be used as a basis for discussion with local officials responsible for water supplies.

### G1.5.2  Rural water supplies — Summary

The Manual gives forms to help in summarising the information gathered at regional and district levels on water resources and the technologies currently used to abstract the water (M1.5.2).

**B**

**G1**

### G1.5.3  Operation and maintenance of rural water supplies

Obviously, it is essential that handpumps and other types of water supply facilities continue to function after they have been constructed. Some form of operation and maintenance (O&M) system should have been established to enable this to happen. As part of the exercise of information gathering and analysis, it is necessary to assess how well the O&M system is working. If no formal system was established, information on the informal maintenance arrangements should be gathered. The methodology proposed (M1.5.3) is based on and adapted from Cotton *et al.* (1994).

The method is divided into two parts. During the fieldwork, information needs to be collected on various aspects of the O&M system at regional, district and village levels. A number of forms are provided for recording this information is a systematic way. This will be assessed in the Analysis section to establish a number of performance indicators for the O&M system.

#### *O&M management systems*

Firstly, it is necessary to categorise the type of operation and maintenance system which is in place. There are a number of ways of organising O&M management. The essential differences relate to the degree of involvement of the user community, the role of the public institutions and levels of government, and the role of the private sector. For practical purposes, systems can be classified into three categories, although in practice systems may be anywhere in a range between them:

VLOM:   Village Level Operation and Maintenance (and Management):
All routine inspections and minor repairs are carried out by trained people from the community, often known as caretakers or village maintenance workers. There is a mechanism for support, and the reporting of and repair of major faults. There is minimum intervention by external agencies.

Area-mechanic maintenance:
A trained, locally based mechanic carries out repairs, involving the community to a greater or lesser extent.

Centralised maintenance:
A team of trained technicians travel out from a depot to inspect and repair facilities. Communities have little if any input apart from sending requests for repairs to be done. It is most common for the public sector to provide this service, although the private sector may be involved.

■ What type of O&M system is in place?

| | |
|---|---|
| VLOM | ☐ |
| Area-mechanic maintenance | ☐ |
| Centralised maintenance | ☐ |
| No formal system | ☐ |
| Other arrangement | |

### *Performance indicators*

To enable the performance of the operation and maintenance system to be monitored and managed, a number of indicators have been developed. These have been adapted for this manual so that an assessment of the current performance of the operation and maintenance system can be made and any problems identified. The performance and problems will later be analysed in the Planning Workshop to improve any deficiencies in the O&M system.

The performance indicators (PI) are divided into groups:

- service
- financial
- personnel
- materials
- work order control

More explanation of each of these PIs is given in Information and data analysis (G2.2.4 and M2.2.4)

Forms for collecting the information and data that will be used to calculate these PIs are given in the Manual (M1.5.3). These should be copied and one completed for each district, and then collated for the region. **It is important to check and verify the information given by district offices during the sample survey of villages.**

B

## G1.5.4 Community pumps: The users' views

G1

It is important to understand how pumps and pump technology work from the users' point of view. Issues to be explored during the Village consultation and surveys include:

- ownership
- how they operate and maintain the pump
- how they get support and assistance if required
- sources and availability of spare parts
- how much it costs them to run the pump
- if a motorised pump, how they obtain and pay for fuel/electricity and lubricants

For each individual village with a pump, the villagers and pump users should be asked for this information. Forms to collect this information in each village are given in the Manual (Forms M1.5.3A and B and Form M1.6.6).

**B**

**G1**

## G1.6  Village consultation and survey

It has been widely recognised in the past decade or so that users themselves should be fully involved in any projects which affect them. There may be limitations on how much they can be involved in designing a programme, but to inform the planning and design process it is essential to gather at village level as much information about the conditions that the beneficiaries themselves face in their lives. They should be enabled to voice their ideas, opinions and problems, and what they themselves define as their needs.

### G1.6.1  Selection  of villages

Obviously it is impossible to visit every village and community in the area, so it will be necessary to choose a representative sample. The actual number of villages to select depends on a number of factors. If the programme area is complex socially, ethnically or geographically, then more villages will have to be covered than if the area is fairly uniform. This has already been considered in outline in the Preparation Phase (MA7) in order to plan the overall time needed to carry out the Preparation Project. Now it is necessary to consider this in more detail and to adjust the original estimate if necessary.

The Manual provides a way of calculating the number of villages that need to be included in the sample survey for each district (M1.6.1).  This takes into account the social and geographic complexity of the area, including factors such as the number of ethnic groups, the topography, use of surface water or groundwater, and use of improved or traditional water supplies.

The actual selection of villages is best done in consultation with district officials during the District-level consultation and surveys. If it has to be done in advance in order to give time to inform villagers of the intended visit, criteria for selection can be drawn up and sent to the districts for them to make the selection.

**B**

**G1**

*Time required*

At least two days in each village should be allowed to carry out the consultation and survey. Time to travel to and from the each village should be added. If it is feasible, the survey team staying overnight in the village would help to build confidence with the villagers, which could result in better information and understanding.

*Team for survey*

The team to carry out the village consultation and surveys should include local staff from the district concerned. Possible staff include:

- community worker or extension agent
- water and sanitation engineer or hydrogeologist
- health worker
- teacher
- agricultural extension agent

## G1.6.2 Participatory process and methods

There are a number of subjects that need to be understood from the communities' points of view for the programme planning and design. To enable communities to be fully involved in their own development, the concept of Participatory Rural Appraisal (PRA) has evolved as one possible approach. A number of exercises and methodologies have been designed for this, some of which will be appropriate for obtaining the views of a sample of villages. These include:

- Semi-structured interviewing
- Key informant interviews
- Group interviews
- Focus group discussions
- Mapping
- Seasonal calendars
- Pocket charts
- Observation
- Environmental tours

An explanation of participatory processes and details of the relevant methods are given in the Manual (M1.6.2).

**B**

**G1**

### G1.6.3  Village survey issues and methods

Table G1.6.3 shows the subject areas, with key points for each subject, and possible methods to use to obtain this information. The application of these is shown in the Manual (M1.6.3), together with fuller explanations and forms for recording the information gathered, as follows:

M1.6.4    General background information on village

M1.6.5    Village water supplies

M1.6.6    Community pumps

M1.6.7    Village sanitation

M1.6.8    Community participation

M1.6.9    Health and hygiene beliefs and behaviour

M1.6.10  Group discussions

M1.6.11  Community health and beliefs

M1.6.12  Hygiene behaviour

B

G1

**B**

**G1**

### Table G1.6.3: Subject areas to understand from communities' point of view

| Subject | Key points | Methods |
|---|---|---|
| Water resources | <ul><li>sources of water</li><li>management of water in community and area</li><li>water rights</li><li>types of water technology in village</li><li>floods and droughts</li><li>seasonal</li></ul> | <ul><li>interviews with key informants</li><li>observation</li><li>environmental tour</li><li>mapping</li><li>seasonal calendar of water source availability and use</li></ul> |
| Water use | <ul><li>uses of water</li><li>quantities of water</li><li>allocation for different uses and priorities</li><li>future plans for water exploitation</li></ul> | <ul><li>focus group discussions</li><li>observations</li><li>questionnaire</li></ul> |
| Maintenance | <ul><li>system of maintenance</li><li>water and sanitation committees</li><li>who carries out maintenance and repairs</li><li>cost sharing/recovery</li><li>reliability of water point</li></ul> | <ul><li>interviews with key informants</li><li>questionnaire</li></ul> |
| Health, hygiene and diseases | <ul><li>community health</li><li>community beliefs about health and disease</li><li>hygiene behaviours</li><li>domestic environment</li><li>use of water</li></ul> | <ul><li>focus group discussions</li><li>checklists</li><li>observation</li><li>interviews with key informants</li><li>seasonal calendar of diseases</li></ul> |
| Sanitation | <ul><li>understanding of sanitation</li><li>present practice regarding defecation</li><li>number and type of latrines in village</li><li>use of latrines, condition</li><li>solid waste</li></ul> | <ul><li>focus group discussion</li><li>observation</li><li>environmental tour</li><li>interviews with key informants</li><li>mapping</li><li>three pile sorting</li></ul> |
| Socio-economics | <ul><li>number of people (disaggregated by gender, age, social grouping)</li><li>number of households</li><li>occupations, incomes and assets</li><li>social organisations and groups, leadership</li><li>gender issues</li><li>educational levels</li><li>clinic or health post</li><li>primary and/or secondary school</li></ul> | <ul><li>focus group discussions</li><li>interviews with key informants</li></ul> |
| Environment | <ul><li>deforestation</li><li>soil condition, soil erosion</li><li>wastewater drainage</li><li>pollution of water resources and sources</li><li>land use</li></ul> | <ul><li>focus group discussion</li><li>environmental tour with community members</li></ul> |
| Community-defined needs and problems | | <ul><li>focus group discussions</li></ul> |
| Interest in water and sanitation programme | <ul><li>priority in list of needs/problems</li><li>willingness to manage planning and implementation of village project</li><li>willingness to contribute to construction (time, labour, materials, money)</li><li>willingness to pay for O&M</li></ul> | <ul><li>focus group discussions</li></ul> |
| Community participation (experience and potential) | <ul><li>previous village projects</li><li>future development plans</li></ul> | <ul><li>focus group discussions</li><li>observation of previous projects</li></ul> |

## G1.7  Village needs assessment workshops

The purpose of these workshops is to enable the views of communities, including their own perceptions of issues and problems and solutions, to be prepared for inclusion in the Planning Workshop.

The participants of the workshops should be representatives from each of the villages that are visited during the village survey and consultation. Each village should send two or three representatives, including at least one woman. In case any representatives are unable to read easily, it may be necessary to provide helpers to assist with the written material in the workshop.

The workshop itself takes one day, with one or two days for preparation in advance. It is suggested that one workshop is held in each district.

A methodology for organising and running these workshops is provided in the Manual (M1.7).

**B**

**G1**

**B**

**G1**

# Stage 2:
# Assessment and analysis

**B**

## Objective of Stage 2

To produce a draft outline programme based on a thorough assessment, analysis and understanding of the programme area and the issues and challenges in the water supply, sanitation and hygiene promotion sector.

## Introduction

The information and data that has been gathered has to be processed and analysed. There are several parts to this, as shown in the Flowchart of Stage 2.

**Data processing (2.1 on Flowchart)** is the numerical analysis of statistical information. The processed data may summarised for presentation during the Planning Workshop.

**Information and data analysis (2.2)** is the assembly and comparison of data and information from different sources, in order to understand particular issues and identify potential problems. The information, data and analysis is summarised for presentation and recorded for use in the various reports that will be prepared as part of the Preparation Project.

The summaries are prepared for presentation in the **Planning Workshop (2.3)**. This participatory workshop is the core of the whole planning process. Representatives from the various different levels (including villages) and various areas of expertise should be invited to this workshop. The workshop uses participatory methods such as problem identification and problem tree analysis to set objectives in each of the areas, and SWOT analysis to look at the institutions in the sector.

The output from the workshop is then **reviewed (2.4)** and compared with the original Terms of Reference for the Preparation Project. A **report** should be prepared for submission to the relevant authority for a decision on whether or not to continue to Stage 3: Programme Design.

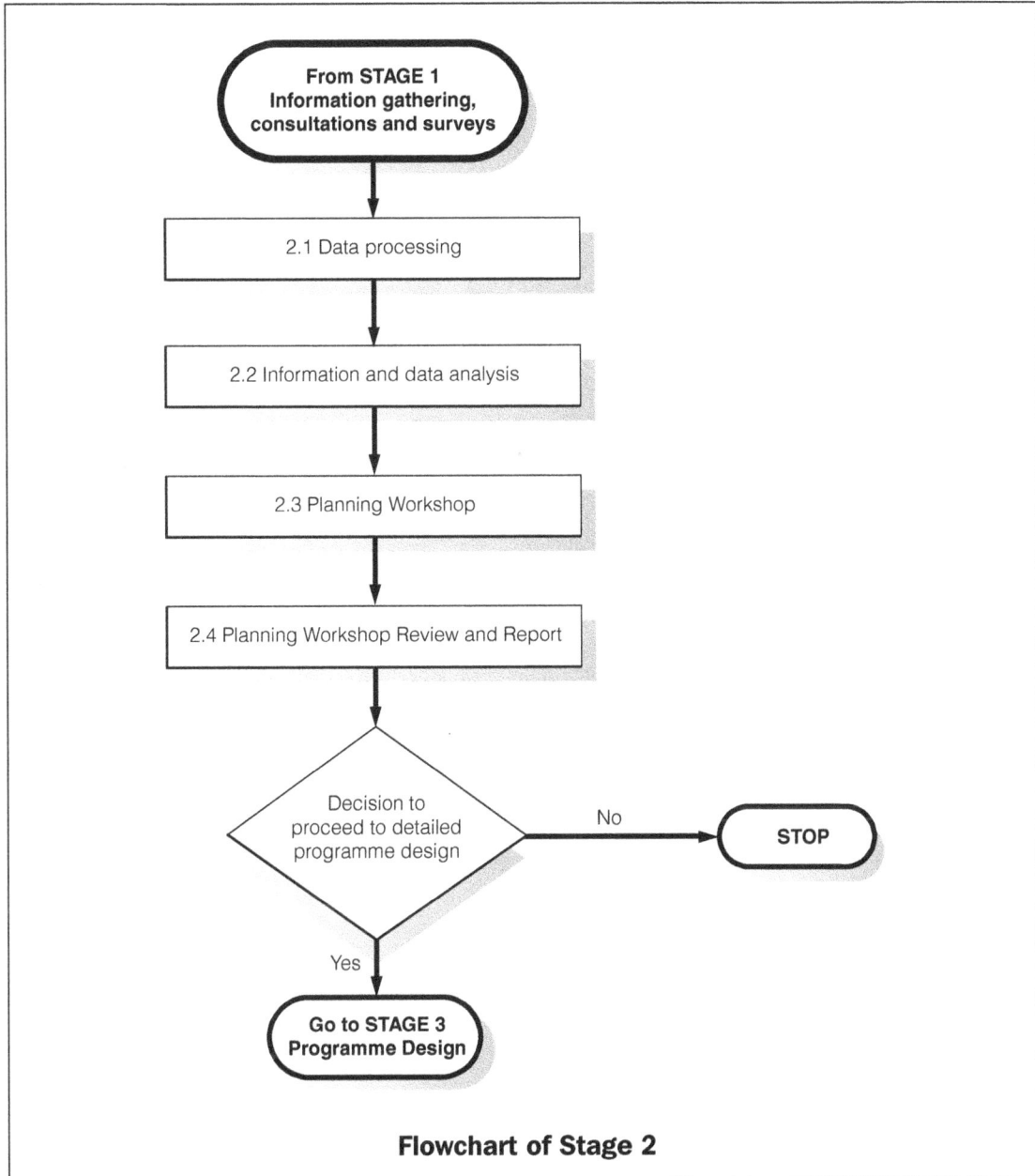

From STAGE 1
Information gathering,
consultations and surveys

2.1 Data processing

2.2 Information and data analysis

2.3 Planning Workshop

2.4 Planning Workshop Review and Report

Decision to proceed to detailed programme design

No → STOP

Yes

Go to STAGE 3
Programme Design

**Flowchart of Stage 2**

B

G2

**Assessment and analysis**                                                    **61**

B

G2

**Assessment and analysis**

# G2.1  Data processing

### G2.1.1  Population data
The basic source of information should be the most recent census. Important things to draw out of the data are the statistics for:

- total population
- population by district
- population by gender and age
- urban and rural populations
- population densities
- households
- female-headed households

To be able to compare data from different sources it will be necessary to bring them to a common date. The most important comparison will be present population with present coverage of water supply and sanitation. It is likely that the latter figures will be the most recent, so population data will have to be increased by the growth rate with any significant changes such as migration or refugee influxes. It will then be necessary to project figures forward for planning purposes.

Thus two sets of calculations will be needed. Spreadsheets for these calculations are given in the Manual (Forms M2.1.1A and B). These can either be photocopied and used to make the calculations manually, or they can entered into a computerised spreadsheet programme such as Excel or Lotus 1-2-3 with the formulæ for automatic calculation.

These will be crude calculations that do not take account of factors such as changes in disease patterns, for example reduction in mortality rates as a result of improved water supply and sanitation. For present planning purposes, however, they are probably adequate.

B

G2

### G2.1.2 Finance

One way of checking whether or not a programme is integrated is to look at the allocation of budgets from all the agencies involved in the sector, including the community contributions in terms of cash, labour and materials, and the private sector. If it is possible from the data collected, it is useful to classify the total amounts of money allocated to and dispersed to the following categories:

- Water supply
  - new construction
  - rehabilitation
  - operation and maintenance
- Sanitation
  - promotion
  - construction of latrines
  - solid waste
- Community organisation, mobilisation and training
- Hygiene promotion
- Water resource management

There may be other categories if the information is already organised in that way. For example, training, transport capital costs and transport running costs may be shown separately, but it is more useful if these can be assigned to the particular component in the main list.

The source of the funding may also be important. It is useful to distinguish between funds generated from the community, funds from local and national sources, and international donor funding. This can indicate the reliance on, and possible vulnerability to, one funder.

Forms for compiling and analysing this information are provided in the Manual (M2.1.2).

### G2.1.3  Coverage of water supply and sanitation

The processing of this data will depend on the way the different organisations define and present their figures. If there is wide variation in the figures and they cannot be reconciled — or if figures are not easily available — it may be necessary to present these variations. These cases could be highlighted as problems for the Planning Workshop to consider.

The easiest way to present this sort of information is to tabulate it. It is useful to present figures as both actual numbers and as percentages of the total number of people or households. It may also be important to distinguish between systems that are operational and systems that have broken down or are in need of rehabilitation.

Possible categories to distinguish levels of coverage could be:

- types of water supply — improved and traditional unprotected sources
- distance to source
- types of latrine

Figures for coverage should be updated to include construction since the figures were produced. This can be done simply by adding the construction or implementation figures for each year to the official figure. Care should be taken that these are *actual* construction, not what was planned.

An example of the presentation of water supply coverage taken from the First Pilot Study of these Guidelines in Zimbabwe is in the Manual (M2.1.3).

**B**

**G2**

### G2.1.4  Disease statistics

Disease statistics gathered from central, regional and district offices and from village health posts is best tabulated so that patterns can be seen and interpretations made. Tables for this are provided in the Manual (M2.1.4). Data gathered from the communities in villages is not statistically valid and should be processed and analysed in a different way. Forms are provided in Manual (M2.1.5).

Important points to bring out of the data include:

- the number of the top ten diseases of adults listed that are water- and sanitation-related;
- the number of the top ten diseases of children listed that are water- and sanitation-related;
- infant and under-5 mortality rates;
- any variations between national and regional figures, between regional and district, and between districts; and
- any variations in percentage terms between village health posts and district figures.

Care should to be taken with data and statistics for several reasons:

- The data for adults and children may not be disaggregated but lumped together.
- It is likely that health data collected from institutions, e.g. health clinics and hospitals, under-estimate the true disease incidence, as these figures only record the cases which have attended clinics and hospitals.
- Health data issued by governments and other organisations may differ and a range of figures may be available, e.g. it is common to see different estimates of infant mortality rates for the same population.
- Health data may be available as actual numbers of cases rather than in the form of rates.

**B**

**G2**

## G2.2 Information and data analysis

A number of issues need to be considered when planning a rural water supply, sanitation and hygiene promotion programme. These issues are inter-related — solutions to one cannot be developed without considering the others. The complexity of these inter-relationships is shown as a matrix in Table G2.2.

The inter-relationships of these issues emphasise the need for integrating the planning and implementation of rural water supply and sanitation programmes. This is not easy to achieve. A number of different professional disciplines are involved. They are not disciplines that naturally relate to or understand each other — especially technicians (engineers and hydrogeologist/ hydrologists) with social development people. The separation of responsibilities into different government ministries also complicates the process.

Information and data analysis involves assembling and comparing data and information from different sources, by different specialists, in order to understand particular issues and identify potential problems.

There are three phases to understanding a complex subject[1]:

- simplistic — when everything seems obvious
- complex — as the implications sink in
- simple again — when insight tames the complications

Guidance on some of the relationships shown in Table G2.2 is given in the rest of this section and the corresponding section in the Manual. Other relationships, for which guidance is not provided, are indicated for the user to think about.

B

G2

---

[1] paraphrased from Chambers, 1993

**Assessment and analysis**                                                                                    **67**

**B**

**G2**

## Table G2.2: Information and data analysis matrix

The shaded boxes show relationships where a decision on an output requires analysis of a variety of types of information and data.

| Output | Plans | Policies | Procedures | Social Economic — population | wealth/poverty | community organisations, structures, committees | community organisation/ development methodologies | Water supply — coverage | operation and maintenance status | technologies | Water resources — hydrology data | groundwater data | Sanitation — coverage | technologies | Hygiene — knowledge, attitudes and practice (KAPs) | h/h education implementation | Organisations — types | specialist areas | finance and budgets |
|---|---|---|---|---|---|---|---|---|---|---|---|---|---|---|---|---|---|---|---|
| **Social economic** | | | | | | | | | | | | | | | | | | | |
| wealth/poverty | ■ | | | ■ | | | | ■ | | ■ | | | | | ■ | ■ | | | ■ |
| community organisation and development methodologies | ■ | ■ | | | | ■ | | | ■ | | | | | | ■ | | | | |
| **Water supply** | | | | | | | | | | | | | | | | | | | |
| coverage and targets | ■ | | | ■ | | | | | | | | | | | | | | | ■ |
| water demand | | | | ■ | | | | | | ■ | ■ | ■ | | | | | | | |
| operation and maintenance | | | ■ | | | ■ | | | | | ■ | | | | | | | | ■ |
| technology choices | | | | | ■ | | | | | | ■ | | ■ | | | | | | |
| **Water resources** | | | | | | | | | | | | | ■ | | | | | | |
| groundwater potential/limitations | | | | | | | | ■ | | | | | | | | | | | |
| surface water potential/limitations | | | | | | | | ■ | | | | | | | | | | | |
| **Sanitation** | | | | | | | | | | | | | | | | | | | |
| coverage and targets | | | | | ■ | | | | | | | ■ | | ■ | ■ | ■ | | ■ | ■ |
| technology choices | | | | | | | | | | ■ | | | | | | | | | ■ |
| **Health/hygiene** | | | | | | | | | | | | | | | | | | | |
| h/h education effectiveness/needs | | | | | | ■ | | | | | | | | | | ■ | | | |
| **Organisations** | | | | | | | | | | | | | | | | | | | |
| implementation capacity | ■ | | | | | | | | | ■ | | | | | | | | ■ | ■ |
| finance | | ■ | | | | | | | | | | | | ■ | | | | | ■ |

**68**                                                                 **Assessment and analysis**

### G2.2.1 Policies, plans and procedures

The various policies, plans and procedures should be read and analysed to understand the implications of anything that may be relevant to the water and sanitation sector.

**Questions to help analysis:**

- What is the implication of the policies, plans and procedures for the sector?
- Will any roles, procedures or implementation arrangements have to be changed?
- Are there any limitations or restrictions on the way things can be done?
- Do the policies, plans and procedures reflect the current thinking in the sector internationally on things like the integration of components, community management and cost recovery? Some of these are discussed in G2.4.7.

#### Policies

From the various policies that have been gathered, abstract anything relevant to the water and sanitation sector. Particular things to note are:

- water resources
- water supply
- sanitation
- health which is relevant to water or sanitation diseases
- health or hygiene education
- social development
- economics related to the sector
- NGOs' roles in the sector and generally

#### Plans

Plans can be classified as general government plans covering all sectors (e.g. a five-year plan, rolling plans) or as sector-specific.

The **general plans** should be analysed in the same way as policies, abstracting the parts relevant to the sector by using the same list as above.

For **sector-specific plans**, abstract:

- the goals;
- objectives;
- targets and coverage figures; and
- definitions and any other information which is relevant or important to consider for the planning of the new programme.

#### Procedures

These should be analysed in the same way as policies, abstracting and summarising the procedures relevant to the sector by using the same list as above. Note anything which creates an enabling environment, or will be restrictive.

**B**

**G2**

### G2.2.2 Interviews[2]

The consultations and surveys at the various levels involved a number of different types of interview. These included:

- individual interviews
- key informant interviews
- group interviews and discussions
- focus group discussions

Analysis of these can be difficult, because of the wide variety of answers, the different points raised by different people, and the length of some of the answers.

A way to analyse the responses is to summarise each interview into the main points raised. From these it may be possible to make a limited number of categories of response that will help to summarise common views and show dissenting views.

It is worth reporting any particularly interesting responses word for word. Any responses raising problems or issues within the water and sanitation sector should be highlighted and written on 'problems cards' for use in the Planning Workshop (see M2.3, Session 4).

**B**

**G2**

---

[2] This is based substantially on part of Tool 1 in Gosling, L., and Edwards, M. (1995)

### G2.2.3  Coverage, targets and implementation capacity

The purpose of this analysis is to establish whether the targets that have been set in the government plans or the Terms of Reference for this programme are realistic and achievable in terms of institutional capacity and finance.

The basic steps to do this are:

1.  Compare the present coverage of water supplies sanitation facilities with the target coverage to establish how much work needs to be done.
2.  Compare the work that needs to be done with the actual present implementation capacity, for software as well as hardware, of the various organisations working in the sector.
3.  Compare the cost of the work that needs to be done with the finance available.

The detailed steps to carry out this analysis are given in the Manual (M2.2.3).

**B**

**G2**

### G2.2.4 Operation and maintenance performance indicators[3]

#### O&M management systems

First, it is necessary to categorise the type of operation and maintenance system that is in place. If there is no system, then the informal arrangements for maintenance should be reviewed. There are a number of ways of organising O&M management. The essential differences relate to the degree of involvement of the user community, the role of the public institutions and tiers of government, and the role of the private sector. For practical purposes, systems can be classified into three categories, although in practice systems may be anywhere in a range between the extremes.

#### VLOM: Village Level Operation and Maintenance (and Management)

All routine inspections and minor repairs are carried out by trained people from the community, often known as caretakers or village maintenance workers. There is a mechanism for support, and for the reporting of and repair of major faults. There is minimum intervention from external agencies.

**Area-mechanic maintenance:** a trained locally based mechanic carries out repairs, involving the community to a greater or lesser extent.

**Centralised maintenance:** a team of trained technicians travel out from a depot to inspect and repair facilities. Communities have little if any input. It is most common for the public sector to provide this service, although the private sector may be involved.

#### O&M performance indicators

To enable the performance of the operation and maintenance system to be monitored and managed, a number of indicators have been developed. These indicators can be used for analysing the current status of the operation and maintenance system to inform the Planning Workshop and prepare the programme design.

During the assessment you should have gathered information which will assist in the calculation and analysis of performance indicators (PIs). The PIs are divided into groups, as shown in Table G2.2.4, with an abbreviation that is used in the survey form (Form M1.5.3A).

#### Table G2.2.4: Performance indicators for operation and maintenance

| • service | S | Functioning water points | number in working order / total number |
| | S | Reliability | functioning time / total elapsed time |
| • financial | F | Cost | average O&M cost per user |
| | F | Revenue | operating revenue / population served |
| | F | Cost recovery | average user payments / average O&M cost per user |
| | F | Subsidy | O&M budget allocation / O&M cost |
| • personnel | P | | |
| • materials | M | | |

The method for calculating the PIs is given in the Manual (M2.2.4).

---

[3] This part is based on and adapted from Cotton *et al.*, (1994), *Tools for the Assessment of Operation and Maintenance Status of Water Supplies*, World Health Organisation, Geneva.

## G2.2.5 Water resources assessment

For readers not familiar with groundwater, an introduction to the subject with a glossary of terms is provided in Appendix A of the Manual.

During the information-gathering process, various pieces of information and data on the water resources in the area should have been collected. To produce an overall assessment of the water resources, water demand and pollution from waste disposal, a number of individual analyses are proposed. These are summarised in Table G2.2.5. Issues to be considered for the individual assessments are given in the Manual (M2.2.5).

Assessments Nos.1 to 6 are to identify the amounts of water available to recharge groundwater in a given area, the amount of runoff and groundwater base-flow available to sustain surface waters, and the variation in likely available volumes and the return periods of extreme conditions of drought and flood. In addition the geographical and geological constraints to the overall water resources potential should be identified.

Assessments Nos.7 and 8 are to identify the levels of existing and projected future demand for water for various uses, and Assessment No.9 is to identify actual and potential pollution from disposal of wastes.

### Table G2.2.5: Water resources assessment

| Assessment No. and title | Scope and use of assessment |
|---|---|
| 1. To derive a conceptual model of the hydrological cycle | Basic understanding of the hydrological cycle enables the water resource potential to be identified in broad terms. It also facilitates technical choice with regard to density and type of water abstraction facility. The assessment presupposes availability of basic climatic data and should be used to provide input to the water resources assessment. |
| 2. To estimate drought and flood return frequency | Annual variation of rainfall in low rainfall areas may be large; it is necessary to appreciate the likely range and the frequency of extreme conditions, as well as current climatic trends. This appreciation is used to enable a sustainable water supply system to be planned that will be capable of withstanding the extremes of climate. |
| 3. To evaluate the geographical constraints | Geographical features affect both hydrology and hydrogeology. Thorough evaluation of these features will identify constraints on surface water and groundwater resources. This evaluation is used for the hydrogeological assessment (Assessment No.5). |
| 4. To evaluate the geological constraints | The geological constraints are the nature and distribution of the various rock types, and the degree and depth of weathering. The information is used to form the basis of a hydrogeological map depicting permeable and impermeable strata and the relative value of one rock type against another for storing and producing groundwater. |
| 5. To bring data together as a hydrogeological assessment | The different levels of data assessed under the three areas of climate, geography and geology can be brought together to form an integrated summary of the available surface water and groundwater resources. This summary is used as the basis for programme design and will inform possible coverage as well as technical choice. It also provides information on where groundwater development is easy and where it is likely to be relatively difficult. |
| 6. To identify shortfalls in data | The data used for the hydrogeological assessment may contain geographical or technical gaps that limit the sensible evaluation of the water resource potential. These should be identified in order to promote future data collection to safeguard the proposed water supply system. |
| 7. To investigate water supply coverage | This identifies the existing patterns and trends in use. It is used to draw on past experience and to identify coverage targets. |
| 8. To assess water abstraction and water use | This assessment attempts to quantify water use in terms of the overall resource. It is used to understand existing patterns of use and trends that are taking place. |
| 9. To evaluate the risk posed by waste disposal to the water resource | This assessment needs to identify the types and volumes of waste material generated and the risk posed by their disposal to the water resource. It is used to see if additional safeguards are necessary to protect the resource. |

### G2.2.6 Assessment summaries

Each member of the planning team who has been carrying out the consultations, surveys and analysis should write a summary of the information gathered and its analysis. This has two purposes:

- to prepare a presentation for the Planning Workshop to give the participants a broad picture of the area and the issues and problems they are dealing with; and
- to make a written record for various reports and programme documents that will be produced.

In addition, each team member should write problem cards for specific problems that they have identified during the consultations, surveys and information analysis.

Table G2.2.6 is a checklist of the information that should be included in the summaries. The summaries should:

- focus on the key points only;
- explain the issues and realities in the programme area;
- bring out important discoveries from the consultation and surveys;
- be presented on flip-chart paper so that the group can refer to them during the course of the workshop; and
- be prepared as handouts for the participants' later reference.

**Table G2.2.6: Checklist for assessment summaries**

| | |
|---|---|
| ☐ | a map of the area, showing features such as rivers and lakes, small towns, mountains, roads, and any important geographical information |
| ☐ | existing coverage of the rural population with water supply facilities |
| ☐ | maintenance status of existing water supplies |
| ☐ | types of traditional source |
| ☐ | types of improved source and method of abstraction |
| ☐ | traditional methods of disposing of faeces |
| ☐ | existing coverage of improved sanitation facilities |
| ☐ | types of improved latrine |
| ☐ | diseases |
| ☐ | official disease statistics |
| ☐ | disease patterns in communities |
| ☐ | people's understanding of the causes of diseases |
| ☐ | key hygiene behaviours and practices |
| ☐ | water resources information |
| ☐ | major uses and allocation of water |
| ☐ | community allocation and use of water |
| ☐ | water rights problems |
| ☐ | total population of area |
| ☐ | rural population of area |
| ☐ | population by gender |
| ☐ | institutions and organisations in sector |
| ☐ | organisational problems and issues |
| ☐ | implementation capacity in each component |
| ☐ | summaries from each Village Needs Assessment Workshop |
| ☐ | successes in past and current projects and programmes |
| ☐ | problems and issues mentioned during the consultation and survey, and arising from the analysis |

## G2.3  The Planning Workshop

The Planning Workshop is the most important part of the process of developing a programme. It enables representatives of all those involved in the programme to work together to explore the issues and problems and to develop solutions. It provides the basis for the detailed programme design. The Planning Workshop should create ownership of the programme by the people who will be responsible for its implementation.

## Objective of the Planning Workshop

To produce a draft outline programme including a goal with the broad objectives, specific objectives and activities necessary for its achievement, by representatives of the organisations and institutions that will be involved in implementing the programme and representatives of the beneficiary communities, based on a thorough understanding of the context in which the programme will operate.

### Process

The process is based on various participatory methods to enable all the participants to contribute. These are outlined in Flowchart 2.3, and each session is described in detail in the Manual (M2.3). Successful conduct of the process depends on having a good facilitator. This person should obviously be experienced in participatory techniques for planning, but should also have some knowledge of the sector and the region.

It may be best to do the workshop in a location away from any of the offices concerned, so that everybody can concentrate on the workshop and not be distracted by other work.

### Time

At least five full days are needed for the workshop, and it may be wise to allow for six days in case extra time is needed. Exercises such as problem tree analysis take considerable time and should not be rushed if the full value of the process is to be realised.

### Participants

Having the right people to participate in the workshop is the key to its success and the success of the resulting programme. Participants should include people involved in the day-to-day issues and problems in the sector, people with detailed knowledge of the issues on the ground, people with specialist and technical expertise, and, most importantly, people whose lives will be affected by the results of the programme — the communities themselves. Thus, representatives should be drawn from:

- communities in each district (selected through the Village Needs Assessment Workshops)
- people who will actually implement the programme that is developed
- district government staff involved in the sector (probably two from each district)
- regional government staff from each concerned department
- central and regional government specialist staff from each concerned department (some of these people may also be from the Core Team)
- the Core Team which has carried out the assessment and analysis part of Stage 2
- decision-makers from key positions within the government system (if they cannot be present, they should be kept fully informed of process and outcomes)
- other specialists involved in the study
- representatives from other organisations involved in the sector, such as NGOs

**B**

**G2**

From 2.2
Assessment and
analysis

**SESSION 1 - Assessment Summary**
Presentations:
Summaries of:
- history of sector
- surveys and consultations
- sample surveys of villages
- village needs assessment workshops
- assessment and analysis

**SESSION 2 - Draft Overall Goal**
based on:
- assessment summaries
- participants knowledge of needs
- participants vision of result of programme
- government's policies and plans

**SESSION 3 - Identification of Successes**

**SESSION 4 - Problem Identification**
in:
- water supply
- water resource management
- sanitation
- hygiene behaviour and practices

from:
- participants' own knowledge and
  understanding
- assessment and analysis
- consultation and survey of various levels
  of government
- village needs assessment workshops

**SESSION 5 - Problem Analysis**
problem tree analysis defining cause and
effect relationships between the problems

turn into

Results to

**SESSION 6 - Specific objectives & activities**
to solve the problems at the various levels
and to continue successful operations

**SESSION 7 - SWOT Analysis of
organisations and institutions**
- strengths
- weaknesses
- opportunities
- threats

problem tree
analysis

**SESSION 8 - Outputs and Activities**
to strengthen organisations and institutions
to achieve objectives and goal

**SESSION 9 - Formulate broad objectives**
- water supply
- water resource management
- sanitation
- hygiene behaviour and practices
- institutional strengthening

Results to

**SESSION 10 - Review of
goal and
objectives**

Do objectives match
draft goal?

Yes

No

Confirm
Overall goal

Adjust draft
goal and
objectives

End of Workshop
Go to 2.4:-
Workshop Review
and Report

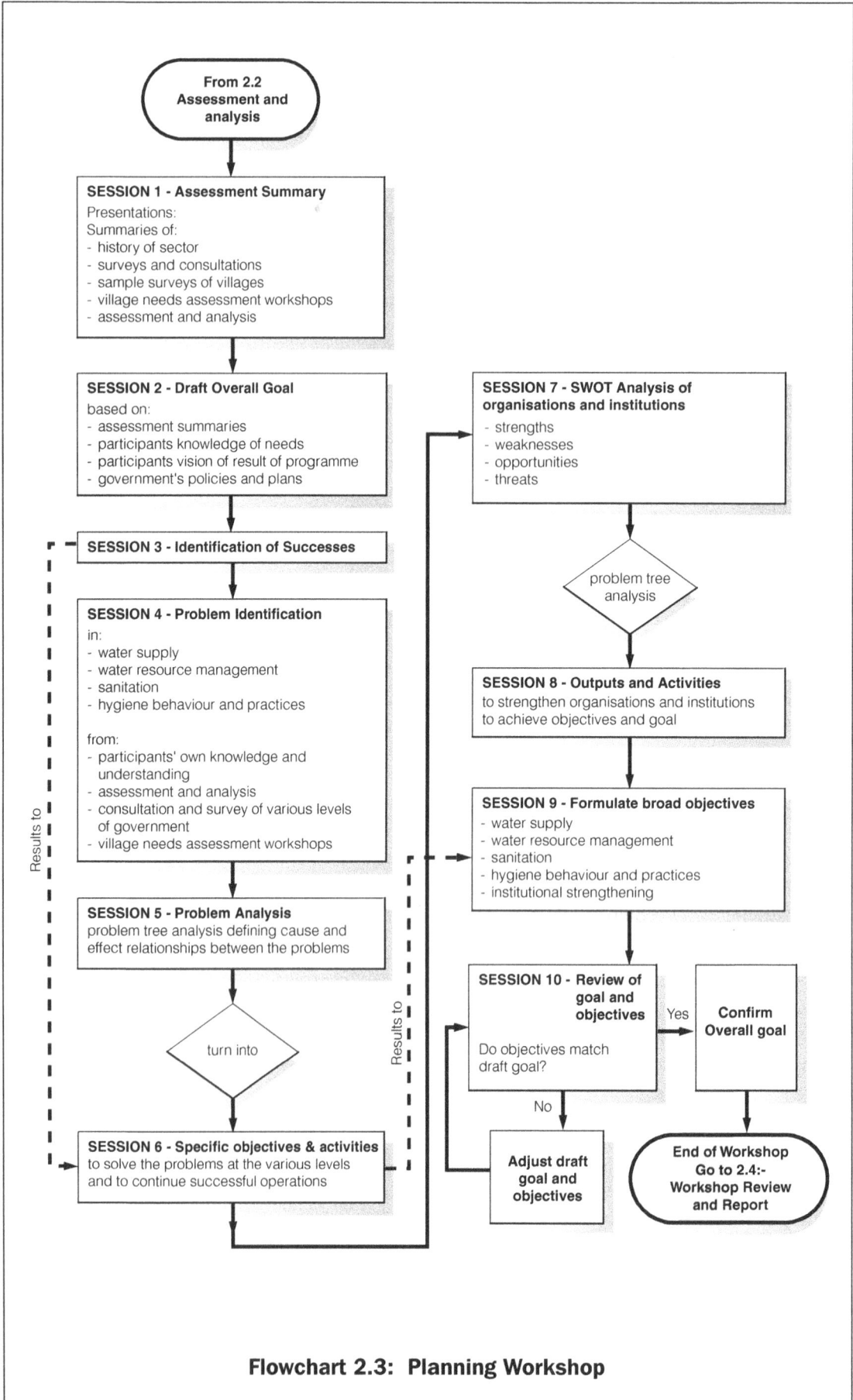

**Flowchart 2.3: Planning Workshop**

## G2.4  Planning Workshop Review and Report

The outputs from the Planning Workshop are solutions to the problems and issues that face the people working in the sector and the communities living in the area. The solutions, in the form of objectives and activities, have been developed by these people. To maintain the participants' ownership of the programme, it is essential to carry these through to the programme design. The format in which they have been presented, however, may make this difficult. Each objective tree is likely to be a mixture of both specific objectives and activities, and they may not be expressed very clearly. The outputs may not cover all the activities and objectives that may be necessary to achieve the broad objective for that component. The Planning Workshop may not have discussed some of the major policy questions facing the sector. This section is to address these issues, leading to the production of a report on which the responsible authority can make a decision to proceed to detailed design of the programme.

## Objective of the Planning Workshop Review and Report

To obtain a decision to proceed to Stage 3: Programme Design based on a report defining a comprehensive outline programme that addresses all the issues, needs and problems in the sector.

### Process

The steps to achieve this are outlined in **Flowchart 2.4**. Master Lists of specific objectives and activities (G2.4.2/3/4/5/6) are the basis of this whole section, and are used at several points. The intention is to capture and maintain the integrity of the outputs from the Planning Workshop but also to ensure that everything that is necessary is included. The sequence of steps is therefore important.

The **outputs** from the Planning Workshop are first **reviewed against the Master Lists** (2.4.1) to record all the points identified by the workshop participants, and to sort them into specific objectives and activities. The sector specialists should then add others from the Master Lists that they consider necessary to achieve the broad objectives in each component.

Decisions have to be made on some **key questions for programme policy** (2.4.7). These are major issues that are currently being discussed in the sector internationally. Based on the results of the decisions, some additional items from the Master Lists may be required, so it is necessary to refer to the lists again.

It is helpful to arrange all the required specific objectives and activities into **objective trees**, showing the hierarchy and relationships between each (2.4.8). These can then be adapted easily to the logical framework format that is required by some donors.

At this stage, a **check back to the original Terms of Reference** for the Preparation Project (2.4.9) will help to ensure that the project is still going in the right direction and achieving what was requested. If it is, a **report of the results of the Preparation Project** (2.4.10) so far should be prepared for the commissioning authority. If the outputs and findings differ from the ToR, it will be necessary to prepare a report to explain why, and propose changes to the ToR if necessary. A decision may then be needed from the commissioning authority on whether or not to accept the proposed changes and proceed to the Programme Design.

**Assessment and analysis**                                                      **77**

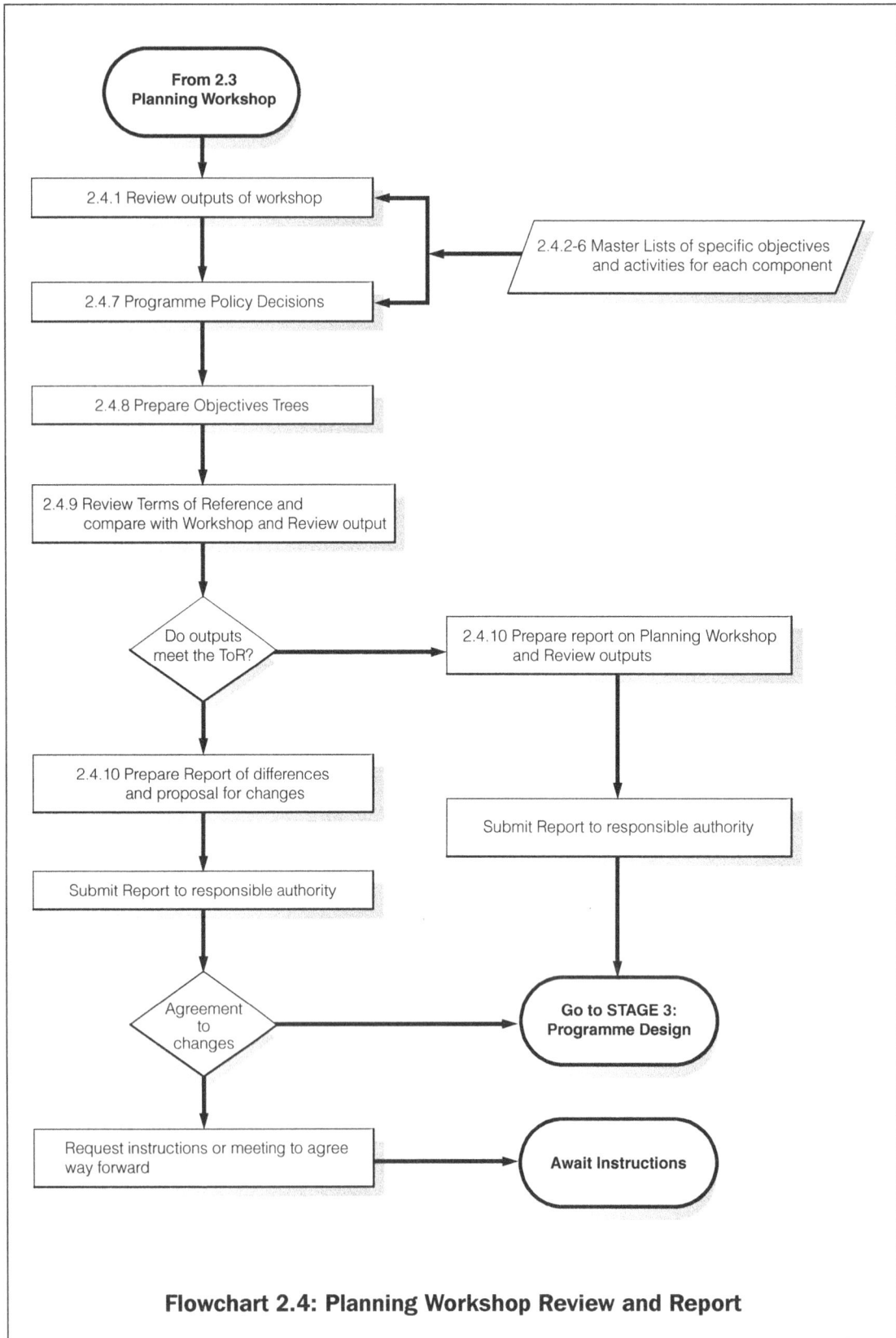

**B**

**G2**

From 2.3
Planning Workshop

2.4.1 Review outputs of workshop

2.4.2-6 Master Lists of specific objectives
and activities for each component

2.4.7 Programme Policy Decisions

2.4.8 Prepare Objectives Trees

2.4.9 Review Terms of Reference and
compare with Workshop and Review output

Do outputs
meet the ToR?

2.4.10 Prepare report on Planning Workshop
and Review outputs

2.4.10 Prepare Report of differences
and proposal for changes

Submit Report to responsible authority

Submit Report to responsible authority

Agreement
to
changes

Go to STAGE 3:
Programme Design

Request instructions or meeting to agree
way forward

Await Instructions

**Flowchart 2.4: Planning Workshop Review and Report**

### G2.4.1 Planning Workshop review

The objective trees from the Planning Workshop are likely to contain a mixture of specific objectives and activities, with no clear distinction between them. In addition, they may not be clearly expressed. The first step is to organise this mixture into a structure for the programme design. Master Lists for each component are provided to assist with this organisation:

G2.4.2   Water supply facilities

G2.4.3   Hygiene promotion

G2.4.4   Sanitation

G2.4.5   Water resource management

G2.4.6   Institution building/strengthening

The next step is to combine these workshop outputs with the professional specialist's own views of the specific objectives and activities needed to achieve each component. This process should be carried out with some care. The output from the workshop is in a sense 'owned' by the participants. Based on their own knowledge, experience and hard work, they have produced what they consider to be the solutions to their problems and the basis for a programme. If done sensitively, it will probably be acceptable to add new material to the output, but not to delete anything or dismiss ideas.

The job of each team specialist is:

■ to review the output
■ to allocate the output into specific objectives and activities, assisted by the Master List
■ to organise the specific objectives and activities so that any gaps can be seen
■ to add additional specific objectives and activities, from the Master List and other relevant information or experience, that are considered necessary

Support on the individual steps is provided in the Manual (M2.4.1).

The following pages contain the Master Lists of specific objectives and activities for each broad objective. The broad objectives, specific objectives and activities are deliberately written in the Lists in a brief summary form. This is so that the users can express these in their own way to suit their programme. A fuller description of all the items in the lists is given in the Manual in Stage 3: Programme Design: Programme components (M3.2).

## G2.4.2  Master List: Water supply facilities

**Broad objective:**  access to safe, adequate and sustainable water supplies

| Specific objectives | Activities |
|---|---|
| WS1  community management of construction of water supply facilities | WS1.1  awareness building |
| | WS1.2  community organisation |
| | WS1.3  establishment of management committee |
| | WS1.4  training for management |
| | WS1.5  training for financial/accounting practice |
| | WS1.6  training for technical skills |
| | WS1.7  scheme selection/prioritisation |
| | WS1.8  technology choice |
| | WS1.9  guidelines for explaining technical/design/financial/procedural matters |
| WS2  construction of water supply facilities | WS2.1  technical choices |
| | WS2.2  standardisation |
| | WS2.3  support organisations (NGOs, private sector) |
| | WS2.4  contracting regulations |
| | WS2.5  quality control |
| | WS2.6  technical support/advice |
| | WS2.7  materials and equipment procurement/provision |
| | WS2.8  finance (including community contribution) |
| | WS2.9  survey |
| | WS2.10  design |
| | WS2.11  accounting/audit |
| | WS2.12  monitoring coverage |
| WS3  rehabilitation of existing water supply facilities | WS3.1  technical choices |
| | WS3.2  standardisation |
| | WS3.3  support organisations (NGOs, private sector) |
| | WS3.4  contracting regulations |
| | WS3.5  quality control |
| | WS3.6  technical support/advice |
| | WS3.7  materials and equipment procurement/provision |
| | WS3.8  finance (including community contribution) |
| | WS3.9  survey |
| | WS3.10  design |
| | WS3.11  accounting/audit |
| | WS3.12  monitoring coverage |
| WS4  system for O&M of water supply facilities | WS4.1  design maintenance system |
| | WS4.2  implement maintenance system |
| | WS4.3  replacement parts supply system |
| | WS4.4  financing |
| | WS4.5  monitoring |
| WS5  community management of O&M of water supply facilities for sustainability | WS5.1  establishment of water user committees |
| | WS5.2  village maintenance workers |
| | WS5.3  training for management |
| | WS5.4  training for financial management |
| | WS5.5  training for technical maintenance skills |
| | WS5.6  operate maintenance system |
| | WS5.7  financing |
| | WS5.8  monitoring |
| | WS5.9  follow-up support to communities |

## G2.4.3  Master List: Hygiene promotion

**Broad objective:**  increased knowledge and improved practices of hygiene and water use behaviour of community, family and individual

| Specific objectives | Activities | |
|---|---|---|
| HP1   hygiene promotion strategy | HP1.1 | review national hygiene education/promotion strategy |
| | HP1.2 | review hygiene education strategies of other countries, NGOs, etc. |
| | HP1.3 | collect information on appropriate approaches for strategy |
| | HP1.4 | design/redesign regional strategy |
| | HP1.5 | increase political commitment to hygiene education at all levels |
| HP2   hygiene promotion | HP2.1 | write guidelines for working practices and training |
| | HP2.2 | develop materials for hygiene promotion |
| | HP2.3 | develop selection criteria and recruit village promoters |
| | HP2.4 | train/retrain village promoters/educators |
| | HP2.5 | monitor performance and impact of training |
| | HP2.6 | community profiles |
| | HP2.7 | baseline KAP surveys and analyses |
| | HP2.8 | identify and prioritise hygiene behaviours for programme to address |
| | HP2.9 | compile village hygiene promotion plan |
| | HP2.10 | hygiene promotion programme implementation |

B

G2

## G2.4.4  Master List: Sanitation

**Broad objective:** access to and use of sanitation facilities

| Specific objectives | Activities | |
|---|---|---|
| SA1  awareness and understanding of need for sanitation by communities | SA1.1 | survey of existing practices and understanding |
| | SA1.2 | development of promotional material, marketing information |
| | SA1.3 | publicity campaigns |
| | SA1.4 | village-level training, workshops, etc. |
| | SA1.5 | demonstration latrines and solid waste disposal |
| SA2  construction of sanitation facilities | SA2.1 | design and standardisation of technologies/ types/costs to offer  choice |
| | SA2.2 | regulations for siting of latrines |
| | SA2.3 | subsidies |
| | SA2.4 | manufacture of components (e.g. latrine slabs) |
| | SA2.5 | training of artisans |
| | SA2.6 | construction of household latrines by individuals/families |
| | SA2.7 | construction of institutional latrines (schools, health posts, clinics, etc.) |
| | SA2.8 | solid waste disposal facilities |
| | SA2.9 | environmental impact assessment |
| | SA2.10 | monitoring of construction numbers |
| SA3  use of facilities | SA3.1 | monitoring of use |
| | SA3.2 | follow-up campaigns |

B

G2

**Assessment and analysis**

## G2.4.5  Master List: Water resource management

**Broad objective:**  management of water resources for sustainability

| Specific objectives | Activities | |
|---|---|---|
| WR1 data collection and monitoring | WR1.1 | identification of data needs |
| | WR1.2 | design and construction of data management system |
| | WR1.3 | collection of baseline data |
| | WR1.4 | collection of historical data |
| | WR1.5 | maintenance of data management system |
| WR2 existing and future demand for water and waste disposal | WR2.1 | evaluate existing water use and waste disposal patterns |
| | WR2.2 | establish trends |
| | WR2.3 | identify causes of water source failure |
| WR3 capacity of water resources | WR3.1 | assessment of groundwater recharge and surface run-off |
| | WR3.2 | assessment of surface and groundwater distribution and availability |
| | WR3.3 | evaluation of water quality and pollution vulnerability |
| | WR3.4 | evaluation of resource sustainability |
| | WR3.5 | identify development potential |
| WR4 sustainable and equitable use of water resources | WR4.1 | establishment of criteria and regulations for abstraction of water |
| | WR4.2 | raising awareness of water resource management with communities, government and other organisations |
| | WR4.3 | allocation of water for various uses |
| | WR4.4 | regulation of water abstraction |
| | WR4.5 | monitoring abstraction and use of water |
| | WR4.6 | management of catchments/recharge zones |
| | WR4.7 | control of pollution |
| | WR4.8 | water rights |

B

G2

### G2.4.6  Master List: Institution building/strengthening

**Broad objective:** the various organisations (government departments, implementing agencies and community organisations) capable of managing and implementing the programme and its projects

| Specific objectives | Activities | |
|---|---|---|
| IS1 policies and procedures | IS1.1 | develop policy, procedures and methodologies for:<br>• village selection procedures/criteria<br>• community management of water supplies (including participation in decision-making)<br>• cost recovery and subsidies<br>• latrine promotion<br>• maintenance (VLOM, private sector or 2/3 tier)<br>• regulation of NGOs<br>• regulation of private sector<br>• responsibility for co-ordination and roles in sector |
| | IS1.2 | implement policies and procedures |
| IS2 management and personnel capabilities | IS2.1 | confirm/redefine/define responsibilities of organisation |
| | IS2.2 | confirm/redefine/define organisational structure |
| | IS2.3 | review and revise job descriptions |
| | IS2.4 | training needs assessment |
| | IS2.5 | source and provide appropriate training |
| | IS2.6 | review/revise staff conditions of service |
| IS3 staff development for community liaison/development/management, hygiene promotion | IS3.1 | employment of social/community development/hygiene education staff |
| | IS3.2 | source or develop orientation and training courses |
| | IS3.3 | training in community organisation, PRA methods, hygiene behaviour and education, etc. |
| IS4 capacity of organisation for implementation/facilitation | IS4.1 | assess implementing/facilitating capacity of organisations (personnel, resources) |
| | IS4.2 | assess needs and targets |
| | IS4.3 | recruit staff |
| | IS4.4 | provide resources |
| | IS4.5 | plan workloads |
| IS5 monitoring and evaluation | IS5.1 | establish monitoring system |
| | IS5.2 | establish monitoring criteria |
| | IS5.3 | establish evaluation criteria |
| | IS5.4 | carry out M&E and use results |
| | IS5.5 | database of existing water supply systems |
| IS6 co-ordination and co-operation | IS6.1 | identification of partner groups (including donors) |
| | IS6.2 | define/confirm lead agency |
| | IS6.3 | registration of implementing agencies |
| | IS6.4 | establishment of co-ordination systems |

### G2.4.7 Programme policy decisions

A number of key decisions on programme policy should be considered at this stage. These are needed to inform the rest of the programme planning and design. The issues are discussed in the rest of this section, and support for making the decision is provided in the Manual (M2.4.7).

After making decisions on each of these issues, additional specific objectives and activities may become necessary. To assist with this, review the Master Lists and pick any additional specific objectives and activities considered necessary to fulfil the key policy decisions.

#### Ownership

The complex concept of ownership is fundamental to a number of other key decisions.

It is now generally accepted that communities should own their own facilities to ensure maintenance and sustainability. This is partly because governments in many places have realised that they cannot afford to maintain facilities themselves and so have 'transferred' ownership to the users. It is also assumed that if people own something they are more likely to look after it properly.

Experience has shown, however, that asking the community to contribute labour and local materials and then 'handing over' the facilities to them after construction does not in itself achieve this ownership. Perceptions of ownership by the various parties are often quite different, even opposite. Government authorities, NGOs and other agencies assume that if a community requests a water supply system and provides 'community participation' for its construction, the community will consider it to be theirs. In practice, because the planning, decisions, technology, finance and materials have been made or provided by outsiders, people still believe that the facility belongs to the outsider. The external agency is still the official owner, despite handover ceremonies and training courses. Cash contributions to capital costs may help to by creating 'financial' ownership, but questions of affordability and exclusion through poverty need to be considered.

These issues are factors in several of the programme policy decisions, but the starting point is the definition of legal ownership. Do the present government regulations allow communities to legally own the water supply systems, or is legal ownership retained by the state? This will affect the way the programme is designed so a key decision for programme policy has to be made on this point.

#### Implementation strategy

Traditionally, water supply and sanitation projects within water supply and sanitation programmes have been implemented by government agencies, private sector contractors, or NGOs, with varying degrees of community participation. Generally, these have not proved to be sustainable, because the concept of community ownership has not been established. A 'handover' to the community at the end of construction is not enough. To promote the concept of ownership, people have to be in control of the decisions affecting their lives.

To solve this problem, the trend has been to pass more responsibility to communities for participation in construction. The ultimate stage in this is for communities to manage the construction for themselves, either by doing the construction work themselves or by supervising a contractor. Increasingly, it is recognised that the development agency, whether government or NGO, should be a facilitator in this process. They should be enabling communities to manage the planning, construction, and operation and maintenance of the facilities. This is much more than participation, which traditionally has meant communities participating in the development agencies' projects. This has significant implications for the design of the programme. Thus a key programme policy decision has to be made.

### Maintenance system

Operation and maintenance is fundamental for sustainability. The large number of broken down water supplies in many countries is evidence that maintenance has not worked. The maintenance system needs to be considered right from the start of the planning process, not added as an afterthought. Issues such as the affordability for villagers to pay for the O&M, and hence the correct choice of technology, are essential. The current maintenance system should already have been assessed during the consultation, survey and analysis stage and analysed during the Planning Workshop. This should indicate whether the current system is working adequately and is affordable. If the maintenance system, whether centralised, three-tier, two-tier or VLOM, is found to be working inadequately, a key programme policy decision will be needed to consider the alternatives.

### Cost sharing

The term 'cost recovery' is often used to mean contributions by communities for water supply and sanitation facilities. The expression 'cost sharing' is used here as a more accurate representation of what is actually meant.

It is now generally accepted that projects should respond to requests from communities for improved services, and that communities should contribute to the capital costs by providing local materials and labour and, increasingly, a cash contribution. (It is also generally accepted that communities should pay the whole cost of operation and maintenance.) Recently, the 'demand responsive approach' has extended this concept of request and community contribution so that communities can choose their preferred level of service from a range of options, but have to pay the additional capital cost of a higher level of service. Underlying this is the principle that water is an economic as well as a social good. A useful source of information on this is the recent Mpumalanga Statement: *Financing of Community Water and Sanitation Services* (Mpumalanga Workshop, 1999).

A risk in this approach is that with the emphasis on the economic aspects, the poorest people will be further marginalised — projects will tend to go to richer communities that can afford to pay for them. Richer communities tend to be able to vocalise their demands better. It may be necessary to facilitate the demand from poorer or marginalised groups in society. The approach is also based on the assumption that there is sufficient water to allow choice. In many countries, water for all uses is becoming increasingly scarce. The choice of higher levels of service for one community that can afford to pay for it may mean insufficient water for another poorer community.

The approach advocated in *Vision 21: A Shared Vision for Hygiene, Sanitation and Water Supply* is that a dialogue must be started with users and communities at the initial stages of projects, on levels of service, tariffs, revenue collection and administration of services. If decision-making is placed close to the community, the resulting costs of water, sanitation and hygiene services can be significantly reduced. This will result in figures far lower than those assumed so far. Leveraging community resources will reduce direct costs, distribute costs among many partners, reduce costs of centrally managed systems, and discourage corruption (Water Supply & Sanitation Collaborative Council, 2000).

Discussion of willingness to pay should distinguish between needs and demands. Equitable financing and cost sharing are essential to enable services for the unserved, and particularly for the poor. Considerations of equity must be balanced with those of financial viability. Neither old dogmas about providing water and sanitation for free, or new dogmas about always charging full cost pricing, are adequate. Charges must be in line with the capacity of people to pay, especially of the poor. Options of payment in kind or in cash need to be considered (*ibid.*).

A key programme policy decision should be made on the process and means to enable all people to have access to a sufficient and affordable water supply.

### Subsidies

A key programme policy decision has to be made on the levels of subsidies for water supply construction and for latrine construction. The subsidy for water supply is tied to the other aspects of cost sharing discussed earlier. Subsidy for latrines is a difficult issue. It is now generally accepted that if subsidies are to be provided, they should only be for the substructure (the latrine slab and the pit lining if required), and that families should provide their own superstructure or housing. If the cost of latrines to the individual family is too expensive, people will not construct them. If the level of subsidy is too high, governments and donors cannot afford to provide it for the numbers of latrines required (ideally one per family for the total number of families in the area).

### Responsibilities of agencies

Responsibility for the various components of programmes is often not clear. For some components, more than one government department claims responsibility, while other components fall in between departments, with none having the responsibility assigned. In the latter case, sanitation promotion is frequently the casualty. A programme policy decision should be made, clearly assigning responsibility for the various components of the programme.

### Co-ordination

Along with clear responsibility for each component, co-ordination to make sure the various components work together is essential. A programme policy decision has to be made to define the lead agency to take on this co-ordination role at each administrative level.

**B**

**G2**

## G2.4.8 Objective trees

Now that all the objectives and activities necessary for the programme have been identified, they can be assembled into objective trees to show the hierarchy and relationships between them.

The trees provided in the Manual (M2.4.8) can be used as a guide for this. The trees should show:

- how the sets of activities together lead to the achievement of the specific objectives; and
- how the specific objectives in turn combine to achieve the broad objectives.

Check to see that the objective/activity set at one level is sufficient to achieve the objective/activity at the next higher level (working upwards on the tree), so that 'doing *this* will lead to achievement of *that*'.

These trees should form part of the Workshop Review Report.

If logical frameworks are used for planning, as required by some donors (including DFID), these objectives trees can easily be converted to that format.

**B**

**G2**

**Assessment and analysis**

## G2.4.9  Review of Terms of Reference

Before proceeding into the Programme Design of Stage 3, it may be important to obtain approval for the scope and scale of the outline programme that has been developed so far. Such approval is likely to be based on how well the Terms of Reference for the Preparation Project are being met. Therefore a review of the outline design against the Terms of Reference is probably necessary.

There are two basic interrelated questions to ask in this review:

- How well does the programme match the ToR?
- Are the ToR relevant to the conditions in the programme area?

If the answer to the first question is that there is a major variance, then the answer to the second question will have to show why these variances are necessary. The ToR would have been written with a limited knowledge of the programme area; the outline programme should be based on the realities in the programme area. It may be necessary to convince the senior decision-makers and politicians of these realities in order to obtain approval of the outline programme and a decision to proceed to Programme Design.

A format for reviewing the ToR against the outline programme is provided in the Manual (M2.4.9).

**B**

**G2**

### G2.4.10  Planning Workshop Review Report

At this stage it will probably be necessary to prepare a report for the commissioning authorities. The purpose of this is to provide information on the progress of the Preparation Project, and to record the outputs so far, including the information assessment and analysis, the outputs from the Planning Workshop and the outline programme from the Planning Workshop Review.

Based on the review of the outline programme design against the Terms of Reference for the Preparation Project (G2.4.9), the report may take one of two forms. It will depend on whether the outline programme conforms to the ToR, or if there is a major variance. Suggested structures for both are provided in the Manual (M2.4.10).

**B**

**G2**

**Assessment and analysis**

# Stage 3:
# Programme Design

## Objective of Stage 3

To produce the design for a rural water supply, hygiene promotion and sanitation programme, incorporating water resources management, of the specified area.

## Introduction

The Planning Workshop and the Planning Workshop Review should have produced an outline
design for the programme. This outline now has to be filled out, including defining the various
objectives and activities that have been identified as necessary. The steps for this are shown in the
Flowchart of Stage 3.

The **specific objectives need to be formulated** (**3.1.3**) in SMART terms with indicators for
measuring progress and achievement. The **activities for each specific objective need to be
designed** (**3.1.3**) in outline, with an estimate of the resources required for each.  Support is
provided for both of these in the Programme components (**3.2**).

The **Programme Management** (**3.3**) system has to be designed. A Master List is provided for
this.

A **budget** for the programme has to be prepared.

The whole programme then needs to be described in the **Programme Design Report** (**3.5**) for
submission to the commissioning authorities for approval.

**B**

**G3**

**Programme design**

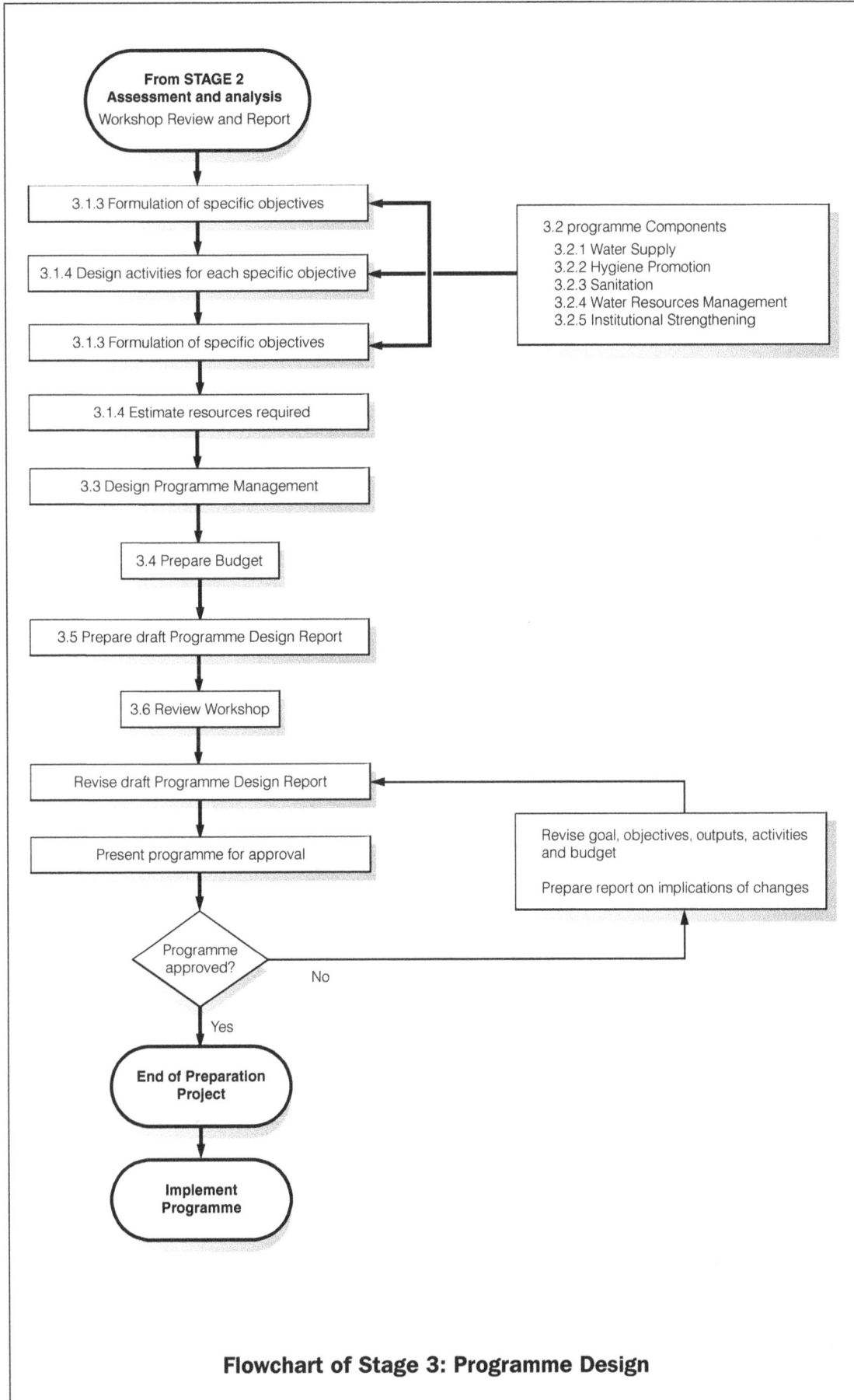

```
        ╭─────────────────────────╮
        │      From STAGE 2        │
        │ Assessment and analysis  │
        │ Workshop Review and Report│
        ╰─────────────────────────╯
                    │
                    ▼
  ┌──────────────────────────────────────┐          ┌──────────────────────────────────────┐
  │ 3.1.3 Formulation of specific objectives│◄────────┤ 3.2 programme Components                │
  └──────────────────────────────────────┘          │   3.2.1 Water Supply                   │
                    │                                 │   3.2.2 Hygiene Promotion              │
                    ▼                                 │   3.2.3 Sanitation                     │
  ┌──────────────────────────────────────┐           │   3.2.4 Water Resources Management     │
  │ 3.1.4 Design activities for each specific objective│◄──────┤   3.2.5 Institutional Strengthening    │
  └──────────────────────────────────────┘           └──────────────────────────────────────┘
                    │                                      │
                    ▼                                      │
  ┌──────────────────────────────────────┐◄───────────────┘
  │ 3.1.3 Formulation of specific objectives│
  └──────────────────────────────────────┘
                    │
                    ▼
  ┌──────────────────────────────────────┐
  │ 3.1.4 Estimate resources required      │
  └──────────────────────────────────────┘
                    │
                    ▼
  ┌──────────────────────────────────────┐
  │ 3.3 Design Programme Management        │
  └──────────────────────────────────────┘
                    │
                    ▼
  ┌──────────────────────────────────────┐
  │ 3.4 Prepare Budget                     │
  └──────────────────────────────────────┘
                    │
                    ▼
  ┌──────────────────────────────────────┐
  │ 3.5 Prepare draft Programme Design Report│
  └──────────────────────────────────────┘
                    │
                    ▼
  ┌──────────────────────────────────────┐
  │ 3.6 Review Workshop                    │
  └──────────────────────────────────────┘
                    │
                    ▼
  ┌──────────────────────────────────────┐◄──────────────────────┐
  │ Revise draft Programme Design Report   │                       │
  └──────────────────────────────────────┘       ┌──────────────────────────────────────┐
                    │                             │ Revise goal, objectives, outputs,      │
                    ▼                             │ activities and budget                  │
  ┌──────────────────────────────────────┐       │                                        │
  │ Present programme for approval         │       │ Prepare report on implications of changes│
  └──────────────────────────────────────┘       └──────────────────────────────────────┘
                    │                                      ▲
                    ▼                                      │
              ╱╲ Programme                                 │
             ╱  ╲ approved? ──── No ──────────────────────┘
             ╲  ╱
              ╲╱
               │ Yes
               ▼
        ╭─────────────────────────╮
        │   End of Preparation     │
        │        Project           │
        ╰─────────────────────────╯
               │
               ▼
        ╭─────────────────────────╮
        │     Implement            │
        │     Programme            │
        ╰─────────────────────────╯
```

**Flowchart of Stage 3: Programme Design**

**B**

**G3**

**Programme design**

## G3.1  Design of programme components

The method described in these Guidelines is for the development of broad strategies for a sector programme, not detailed decisions about specific projects or interventions. This is important to bear in mind during development of the programme design. Options should be selected in terms of overall parameters, mechanisms, systems, processes, criteria, collaborative arrangements, etc., while also narrowing the range of options to ones that are appropriate and based on sound programming principles.

In fact, the need is to plan for flexibility, for enabling the use of a variety of approaches for implementing the programme and projects within it. Each community is unique, and your decisions must help create the means by which communities will be able to make decisions and gather the will, interest and resources to create and sustain a healthier environment. Similarly, regarding the institutional arrangements involved, there are no absolute answers. In some cases it will be necessary to proceed by trial and error, and/or specify what further study is needed to resolve a need or problem that hinders efforts in the water and sanitation sector in the region or country (Environmental Health Project, 1997).

### Process

In the Planning Workshop and the Planning Workshop Review, only the broad objectives have been fully defined in specific, measurable, achievable and time-bound (SMART) terms (see M3.1.1 for detailed explanation). When objectives are clear, it is possible to clarify all the activities of the programme. Clear objectives also enable progress to achievement to be monitored. Indicators for monitoring are an essential part of this. A detailed description of these is given in the Manual (M3.1.3).

The programme design team now has to develop the specific objectives in SMART terms and the activities necessary to achieve those specific objectives. The process is explained in the Manual, with Forms M3.1.1 and M3.1.2 provided to help the design team in this task (M3.1.1 and M3.1.2). To assist with this process, the programme components are described in some detail (M3.2).

### Time planning

A time plan in the form of a Gant Chart (or bar chart) should be prepared in broad terms for the programme period. It should show the main activities under each broad and specific objective. Some guidance on the time and timing for activities is given in Programme components (M3.2).

The time scale is probably best to the nearest quarter — monthly planning at this stage may be too detailed. It may be helpful to show additional information such as seasons, and periods when communities are busy with farming or have time available for projects.

Rate of implementation should be governed by the process needing the most time, usually the social development and development of community capacity to manage. Rates of implementation should also be based on the analysis of capacity of each organisation.

**B**

**G3**

Programme design

## G3.2  Programme components

To assist in the development of the specific objectives and activities of each component of the programme, some of the principles and issues to consider are provided in the Manual (M3.2). These cover:

- Water supply (M3.2.1)
- Hygiene promotion (M3.2.2)
- Sanitation (M3.2.3)
- Water resource management (M3.2.4)
- Institutional strengthening (M3.2.5)

The structure follows the pattern of specific objective and activity. After a discussion of issues at specific objective level, the points to consider for each activity under that specific objective are described. These should be referred to during formulation of the objectives and activities. For some of them, it may also be useful to refer back to the Programme policy decisions (G2.4.7). References are also given for further information on the particular subject.

**B**

**G3**

**B**

**G3**

Programme design

## G3.3  Programme management

One definition of management is getting things done through other people. This is useful for programme management, considering the scope of the programme that is being developed. The definition of programme taken for these Guidelines is:

> a coherent framework of procedures and activities for co-ordinating and regulating projects within the water and sanitation sector in a defined geographical area.

One department or organisation is unlikely to be able to undertake all the activities for improved water supply and sanitation itself. A number of different organisations and different types of organisations have to work together to do it. Thus programme management is getting the activities of the programme done through the various organisations, communities and projects. It involves planning, organising, checking and co-ordinating to ensure that all the organisations work together on the various components to achieve improved, sustainable accessibility to water supply and sanitation facilities for people, leading to the programme goal.

**B**

### G3.3.1  Master List: Programme management

**Broad objective:** Efficient and effective management of the programme to achieve the goal

| Outputs | Activities | | |
|---|---|---|---|
| PM1   integration and coverage of components | PM1.1   planning | | |
| | PM1.2   projects | | |
| | PM1.3   co-ordination | | |
| PM2   regulation of procedures, standards, etc. | PM2.1   implement policies and procedures | | |
| PM3   management of resources | PM3.2   funding — donors, government budgets | | |
| | PM3.2   implementing agencies | | |
| | PM3.3   materials | | |
| PM4   management structure and organisation | PM4.1   define programme structure and organisation | | |
| | PM4.2   manage staffing | | |
| | PM4.3   plan workloads | | |
| PM5   reports | PM5.1   preparation of reports | | |
| PM6   monitoring and evaluation | PM6.1   M&E of policies, procedures, projects, organisations | | |
| | PM6.2   use results to improve projects, procedures | | |
| | PM6.3   advocacy | | |

**G3**

**B**

**G3**

**Programme design**

## G3.4 Budget

Budgeting is as much about planning as it is about finance. Without careful plans, it is impossible to budget; but without budgets, plans cannot be realised and costed effectively. In other words, budgets translate plans and activities into financial terms (Eade and Williams, 1995).

Preparing a budget for a programme over a five- or ten-year time-scale covering a region may not be possible using standard government budget formats. It will probably be easiest to use a 'broad brush' approach, rather than detailed costing of every component.

With the scope and scale of the programme, and the variety and uncertainty of sources and potential sources of funding, it may be worth dividing the budget into two parts[4]:

- a **guaranteed budget** for the expenditures which it is anticipated will be covered, for example, by the annual government budget allocation; and
- a **complementary budget** for additional expenditures which depend on funding which is not yet guaranteed, but which is planned as part of the programme.

Budgets are also generally divided into:

- **capital:** tangible and lasting items such as buildings and equipment; and
- **revenue:** recurrent costs such as payments to staff and suppliers for services and consumable goods.

The government ministries may already have prescribed systems and formats for budgeting, so it is probably best to use these. If they are for annual budgeting, however, they may require too much detail. An alternative may be to look at the system used for things such as rolling plans (e.g. national five-year plans).

B

G3

---

[4] adapted from Eade and Williams (1995)

**B**

**G3**

**Programme design**

## G3.5  Programme Design Report

Until the programme is implemented, the Programme Design Report is the primary product of the Preparation Project. As such it is a very important document. Apart from being used for the implementation, it will be circulated at senior levels in government and to potential donors and other external agencies. Therefore it should be comprehensive but still clear and accessible.

The following is a suggestion for the format and contents of the Programme Report. As far as possible, detailed information and background data should be assigned to Appendices, with only a summary discussion of the pertinent facts in the main body of the report.

### Suggested table of contents

### Summary

### Abbreviations

1. **Introduction**
   - Origin of programme
   - Process of developing programme

2. **Programme area**
   - Geography
   - Demography/population
   - Economy
   - Sources of income
   - Poverty/wealth
   - Gender

3. **Water and sanitation sector analysis**
   - Water
     - water resources
     - policies and regulations
     - allocation by sector
     - types of abstraction
     - coverage of water supply facilities
     - operation and maintenance system
     - operation and maintenance status
     - costs

   - Health/hygiene promotion
     - common diseases
     - morbidity/mortality
     - people's understanding
     - policies and regulations

   - Sanitation
     - policies and regulations
     - types of latrine
     - costs
     - coverage
     - people's understanding and use
     - solid waste disposal
     - wastewater drainage

**B**

**G3**

**B**

- Institutional arrangements
  - national
  - regional
  - district
  - community
  - organisations
    - government
    - donors
    - national NGOs
    - international NGOs
    - private sector
  - planning and co-ordination
  - finance
  - budget allocations
  - donor funds
  - existing programmes and projects
  - plans

### 4.  Programme goal, objectives
- Goal
- Broad objectives
- Specific objectives
- Activities (summary)

### 5.  Scope
- Procedures and regulation
- Water supply construction
- Rehabilitation
- Operation and maintenance
- Sanitation
- Hygiene promotion
- Training
- Institutional strengthening
- Implementation assistance

**G3**

### 6.  Finance
- Summary estimates
- Financing plan
- Community contribution/cost sharing
- Subsidies

### 7.  Implementation arrangements
- Institutional arrangements
- Programme management
- Lead agency
- Co-ordination
- Roles and responsibilities
- Regulations and procedures
- Implementation schedule (bar/Gant chart)
- Operation and maintenance system
- Reporting
- Monitoring
- Evaluation

## 8.   Environmental issues
- Environmental impact assessment

## 9.   Risks
- Identification
- Minimisation

## Appendices
1. Project Preparation study team
2. Terms of Reference
3. References
4. Environmental evaluation
5. Cost estimates — basis of estimates (unit costs)
6. Objective trees
7. Activity sheets

... other detailed information

**B**

**G3**

B

G3

## G3.6  Review Workshop

To ensure that the ownership of the programme is maintained, a second workshop involving all the participants from the Planning Workshop is advised. This is to give these people, who will be implementing and benefiting from the programme, an opportunity to review and discuss how the programme has evolved since their first outline design. It is a chance for them and the programme designers to check that the draft programme is still relevant to address the problems and issues that they face in the sector, which were analysed in the Planning Workshop.

The draft Programme Design Report should be sent to all the participants well in advance of the Review Workshop. This should give them a chance to understand the report and discuss it with colleagues and other stakeholders.

The Review Workshop itself should be planned to take two or three days. A suggested timetable is provided in the Manual (M3.6)

After the Review Workshop, it may be necessary to revise the draft Programme Design Report to take account of changes proposed by the participants, before submitting it to the commissioning authority.

B

G3

**B**

**G3**

# Appendices

Appendices

# Appendix A: Introduction to technical aspects of groundwater development for rural water supply

Groundwater development requires input from many disciplines: economists, sociologists, planners and administrators as well as specialists to address the technical aspects of resource evaluation, water supply design and resources management.

Groundwater development is different in nature to many engineering projects. Data are always incomplete and progress must be cautious and controlled. This Appendix describes the processes involved in developing a groundwater resource and how knowledge of the behaviour of a groundwater system can be improved through sensible management. It is intended to provide only sufficient information for the non-specialist to be able to appreciate the technical input of the hydrogeologist within the Preparation Project. Good groundwater development measures include:

- good, careful management;
- good practices for design and management of work;
- monitoring and databasing; and
- maintenance.

## The stages of development

During the early stages of development, groundwater is frequently used in an *ad hoc* way. Depending on location and need, holes are dug in the ground, springs are exploited, even horizontal drains (used for many centuries by the Arabs, Romans and South American Indians) as well as manually drilled boreholes (as in China and India) may be constructed.

As needs expand, a more detailed investigation or feasibility study of the groundwater system is required before further development can sensibly take place. Estimates are made of the rate at which the aquifer system is replenished by rainfall, and further drilling, perhaps controlled centrally, then proceeds. In due course further development may place the level of extraction close to the replenishable limit of the aquifer and shallower more vulnerable sources may start to dry up seasonally. Artificial recharge, perhaps from rivers, may help alleviate the situation, but this respite may only be temporary. At this stage degradation of the aquifer may progressively occur. Unless extreme care is taken, over-exploitation, often accompanied by deteriorating water quality and pollution of the resource, will begin to take place.

A main objective of the Programme is to avoid placing the available water resources in jeopardy and to avoid degradation of the resource. This will assist the likelihood of developing a sustainable rural water supply system. It can be accomplished through careful planning and assessment.

## Some hydrogeological concepts

Aquifers are reservoirs, and can act as buffers to variations in rainfall and recharge from rainfall, so they are capable of maintaining supply through prolonged dry periods. Groundwater moves through pore spaces or fissures within the saturated part of the aquifer. The aquifer can thus act as a filter to solid material such as waste, but water is also a solvent and it can take some material into solution. A hydrogeologist is able to quantify some of these characteristics. A glossary of technical terms is provided to help in understanding.

## Groundwater hydraulics

Groundwater derives from recharge by rainfall percolating vertically downwards under gravity through the soil zone to reach the water table. In this state the groundwater is unconfined, and once it has reached the water table it may flow laterally according to the prevailing head difference or hydraulic gradient on the water table. It may flow down the hydraulic gradient beneath an impermeable cover, at which point the aquifer becomes confined.

What happens at any one point in a groundwater system may affect what happens at other points. Whether these need to be considered in the ultimate management of the aquifer depend on the distances and time scales involved. If a distance is fixed, such as that between two village wells, then it is the time for a significant effect to propagate across that distance which is important. Conversely if the time scale is fixed, such as the duration of a drought, then the distance that is affected by pumping a source or group of sources becomes significant.

## Groundwater chemistry

Groundwater chemistry is controlled by atmospheric inputs within the rainfall, biological activity mainly within the soil zone, water-rock interaction and human impacts.

Rain is a source of a number of solutes in small quantities and is also a weak acid. Acidity is enhanced in the soil zone where microbial activity promotes production of carbon dioxide ($CO_2$). This acidity in turn drives the weathering and dissolution process at the base of the soil where water and rock interaction and ion exchange are greatest. The presence of carbonate minerals such as calcite either as a sandstone cement, fracture infill or as limestone cause hard, carbonate rich groundwater, whereas silica rich rocks such as granite and silica cemented sandstones cause relatively soft and sometimes slightly acid groundwater.

The percolating groundwater may take only a few hours to pass down a fissure to the water table or it may proceed at a rate of up to 1 metre per year in a porous stratum such as alluvium. Once at the water table it can flow down the hydraulic gradient towards a natural point of discharge (a spring or baseflow discharge to a river or a stream). Depending on the distances, hydraulic gradient and transmissivities involved, this may take between a few tens of years to many thousands of years. The older the groundwater the greater the opportunity for it to reach chemical stability with the solid rock and generally this also means the more mineralised or more saline it can become. Older waters may be zoned with increasing depth, and it is not uncommon to find younger fresher groundwater over older saline (and, therefore, more dense) water.

The presence of oxygen in an unconfined aquifer, or reducing anoxic conditions which may be generated in an unconfined aquifer, dictate the chemical process that may occur within a given rock type. Extreme reducing conditions promote the uptake of metals in solution. These are commonly manifested as ochreous iron-stained deposits derived from the water once it is pumped up and left in contact with the air. Other metals may also be present, notably manganese, and sometimes lead and zinc. World Health Organisation suggests maximum desirable potable levels for various elements in *Guidelines for drinking-water quality: Volume 1 Recommendations* (WHO, 1993).

The main factor affecting transport of pollution through aquifers is the flow rate, which depends on the transmissivity and thickness of the aquifer, and the hydraulic gradient. Other factors to pollutant transport are adsorption on to the mineral grains and biological activity in the soil zone. Some organic pollutants also tend to break down through a process known as biodegradation, and with time change into new, sometimes less harmful products, in terms of water potability. Pollutant transport also affects dilution according to diffusivity within the aquifer. All these factors tend to produce an overestimation of groundwater pollution from point sources. Nevertheless protection of groundwater sources from contamination, particularly from nearby waste disposal facilities, is an important design consideration particularly for shallow and vulnerable unconfined aquifers.

# Hydrogeological glossary

| | |
|---|---|
| *adsorption* | the process by which a thin layer of a substance accumulates on the surface of a solid substance |
| *aerobic* | in the presence of the atmosphere and free oxygen. |
| *aquifer* | a rock formation which is sufficiently permeable to yield a usable quantity of water to a borehole, well or spring |
| *baseflow* | the sustained flow of a stream, provided from stored sources (principally groundwater). The flow is unrelated to a specific rainfall event |
| *biodegradation* | microbial breakdown of a compound |
| *bedrock* | the unweathered rock beneath the saprolite, regolith and/or alluvium |
| *confined aquifer* | an aquifer overlain by less permeable strata in which groundwater is under pressure |
| *crystalline basement* | non-sedimentary rocks which yield water from the regolith or aquifer weathered surface and fractures at depth |
| *drawdown* | the difference between the rest water level (or piezometric head) and the water level caused by pumping a borehole |
| *electrical resistivity depth sounding* | a geophysical survey technique by which an electrical current is passed through the ground between electrodes, and measured via another pair of electrodes. Electrode separation reflects the depth of observation. Interpretation is by mean of analogue |
| *evapotranspiration* | water returned from plants to the atmosphere |
| *fissures / fractures* | the preferential storage and transport of groundwater in fresh bedrock may best occur in dilated cracks or joints. Water may be fed to the fractures from the granular regolith above, provided that the saprolite is saturated |
| *gravel pack* | rounded granular material (typically 1 to 3mm in diameter) placed in the annulus behind slotted borehole casing or screen. It acts as a borehole stabiliser and as a means of promoting water flow into the borehole |
| *groundwater system* | qualitative description of the flow of groundwater in an aquifer and how it is affected by the prevailing geology |
| *head* | the height to which water rises above a set datum (often sea level) in a well or borehole |
| *hydraulic gradient* | the prevailing inclination of the water table which provides the driving force to transmit groundwater through an aquifer |
| *igneous* | rocks formed by solidification from a molten state; includes intrusive (e.g. granites) and extrusive rocks (e.g. lavas) |
| *ion exchange* | the exchange of ions between different colloids |
| *lithology* | a term referring to the general characteristics of a sedimentary rock |
| *metamorphic* | a rock derived from a pre-existing rock by mineralogical, chemical or structural change (e.g. pressure, heat), the process being sufficiently complete to form a well-defined new rock type |
| *permeability* | the ability of a material (e.g. rock) to allow fluid to pass through it under the pressure of a hydraulic gradient |
| *piezometric level* | the level to which water will rise in a borehole which penetrates groundwater confined in a fracture or beneath a confining layer such as clay |
| *porosity* | the ratio of the volume of the voids in a rock to the total volume of the rock |
| *precipitation* | rainfall or snowfall |
| *recovery* | the process which occurs when a pump is stopped and the water level in the borehole is allowed to rise back towards its static pre-pumping level. Incomplete recovery at an elapsed time greater than the total duration of the pumping phase may indicate over pumping |
| *regolith* | the weathering product that may be present over crystalline basement rocks. It may have a clay-rich upper part which inhibits downward percolation of rainwater, and is generally granular, progressing to blocky with depth. It may be a few metres to a few tens of metres thick |
| *salinity* | the concentration of salts and chemicals within water |
| *sedimentary* | a rock that has been laid down under the action of water, wind or ice from the detritus of existing rock material |
| *storativity* | the volume of water that can be removed under gravity from a saturated rock mass |
| *specific capacity* | the yield of a borehole divided by the respective drawdown. For inter-borehole comparison the pumping elapsed time should always be the same (e.g. 240 minutes) |

Appendices

| | |
|---|---|
| *specific electrical conductivity* | the unit electrical conductivity of a fluid, which in the case of groundwater reflects the salinity of the water |
| *storativity* | the volume of water that can be released from or taken into storage per unit surface area of the aquifer for each unit change of head |
| *transmissivity* | a measure of the ability of an aquifer to transmit groundwater, being the product of aquifer thickness and aquifer hydraulic conductivity |
| *unconfined aquifer* | an aquifer in which the saturated zone meets the unsaturated zone at the water table, the latter maintained at atmospheric pressure |

## Bibliography for Water Resources Assessment

- American Society of Civil Engineers (1996)
- Bureau of Reclamation (1997)
- Calow *et al.* (1997)
- Freeze and Cherry (1979)
- Gunston (1998)
- Hamill and Bell (1986)
- Lerner *et al.* (1990)
- Linsley (1981)
- Struckmeier and Margat (1995)
- Todd (1980)
- Twort *et al.* (1985)
- Walton (1970)
- Wilson (1990)
- World Meteorological Organisation (1994)

# Appendix B: Implementor or Facilitator? Achieving Community Management in Nepal[27]

## Jeremy Ockelford and Vijaya Shrestha

In a paper written for WHO, IRC states that 'governments have a vital *facilitating* role to play in fostering local management and control of community water sources and supplies' [emphasis added]. It goes on to emphasise partnership with local communities, and the type of decisions communities should be making with support of government agencies (IRC International Water & Sanitation Centre, 1995). But how are government agencies to achieve this? In many places government departments implement projects and programmes with community participation, but this can mean many different things.

The transformation from implementor to facilitator is much more difficult. This paper looks at a case in Nepal where His Majesty's Government's Department of Water Supply & Sewerage (DWSS) is making major efforts to achieve this transformation. The start of the process of changing this technical department to undertake the social and community components of rural water supply and sanitation were described by Shrestha and Pyakural (1996).

During the preparation of a major rural water supply and sanitation sector loan project with DWSS and the Asian Development Bank in early 1996, there was a debate in the water and sanitation sector about the respective roles of implementor and facilitator. These terms were not clearly defined but there was an assumption that the DWSS was an implementor, which was a bad thing, and that other groups, particularly NGOs, were facilitators, which was a good thing. Implementor and facilitator were seen in black and white terms, with an organisation being either one or the other. In fact, further discussion revealed that in many cases, NGOs had taken over the role of implementor instead of facilitating communities to manage the construction, operation and maintenance of their own water supply systems (Asian Development Bank and Department of Water Supply and Sewerage 1996).

This view of implementor and facilitator is rather simplistic and limiting. There are many steps in a project and in any one of these an agency may be an implementor or a facilitator, or part way between the extremes. To assist the DWSS in its efforts to change its way of working the team of consultants and staff preparing the project developed a table of the extreme definitions for implementor and facilitator in each step of the project, together with the changes needed to move from one to the other. A modified version of this is shown in Table 1 (Asian Development Bank and Department of Water Supply and Sewerage 1996).

The Table does not define the position of any particular agency, but it can be applied to any agency, including NGOs. An agency can be located anywhere at or between the extremes, so it may be a facilitator in some activities and an implementor in others. The DWSS itself was already a facilitator in several of the steps of a project, and was making progress in other steps.

---

[27] Paper reproduced from Ockelford and Shrestha (1998) in Pickford (1998)

# Table 1: Definitions of Facilitator and Implementor

| | Activity | Implementor | Facilitator | Changes needed |
|---|---|---|---|---|
| 1 | Community Water Supply and Sanitation Awareness Campaign | ▪ Telling people about water supply and sanitation | ▪ Participatory discussion, with broad range of people in communities, about water supplies, hygiene and sanitation, drawing out people's own interests, practices and concerns. <br><br> ▪ Explanation of how people will be involved with and make decisions in sub-projects. | ▪ Staff orientation <br><br> ▪ Training in PRA techniques <br><br> ▪ Clear methodology for campaign meetings |
| 2 | Request from community | ▪ Request from small group only <br><br> ▪ Political requests | ▪ Broad based request from many (majority) members of community | ▪ Orientation to DDC Council and Assembly |
| 3 | VDC and DDC Request Approval | ▪ Decisions made without information, transparency or accountability | ▪ Formal approval by VDCs <br><br> ▪ Prioritisation by DDCs in accordance with published criteria <br><br> ▪ Communities informed of prioritisation | ▪ Criteria published <br><br> ▪ Priority criteria explained to communities <br><br> ▪ Transparent decision making |
| 4 | Pre-feasibility study | ▪ Study directed by overseer with support of community | ▪ Use of PRA techniques <br><br> ▪ Mass meetings to provide orientation on project activities and procedures <br><br> ▪ Verifications of need for water and interest of communities <br><br> ▪ Data gathering by and with community members <br><br> ▪ Water source identification <br><br> ▪ Preliminary layout of system by community with technical explanation and advice by overseer | ▪ Training in PRA and community approaches <br><br> ▪ Training in facilitation of meetings <br><br> ▪ Adequate time for processes |
| 5 | DDC and DWSS prioritisation | ▪ Decisions made without information, transparency or accountability | ▪ Prioritisation by DDC/DWSO in accordance with published guidelines and criteria <br><br> ▪ Communities informed of prioritisation and decision | ▪ Clear simple guidelines and criteria openly available <br><br> ▪ Transparent decision making |
| 6 | User need survey & feasibility study – socio-cultural, economic, health, technical | ▪ Survey staff carry out survey asking community for information <br><br> ▪ Technical survey by technician/overseer with help from villagers | ▪ Mass meetings to discuss feasibility study and explain techniques <br><br> ▪ Use of PRA techniques <br><br> ▪ Data gathering by community members <br><br> ▪ Preliminary layout of system by community with technical explanation and advice by overseer <br><br> ▪ | ▪ Training in PRA <br><br> ▪ Survey methodology based on PRA <br><br> ▪ Development of methods and teaching materials to explain technology <br><br> ▪ Change in attitude of technical staff to share and explain engineering knowledge <br><br> ▪ Sufficient time for process to be conducted at villagers' pace |
| 7 | Appraisal of Feasibility Study Report | ▪ Appraisal by agency | ▪ Appraisal by agency and community | ▪ Sufficient time <br><br> ▪ Feasibility report in Nepali and English |

| | Activity | Implementor | Facilitator | Changes needed |
|---|---|---|---|---|
| 8 | Social preparation process | • Communities told about processes and processes imposed | • The following conducted using participatory methodologies:<br>• WUSC formed<br>• Health workers and teachers identified<br>• VMW appointed<br>• Volunteers selected<br>• O&M systems discussed and developed, including payment to VMW and O&M fund | • Sufficient time<br>• Technicians and overseers with community development skills<br>• Participatory methodologies for WUSC formation, VMW appointment, volunteer selection, etc.<br>• Linkage with and support to health posts |
| 9 | Agreement signed<br>WUSC - Agency | • Takes place between WUSC Chair and DE at DWSO, or at Agency's office | • Mass meeting to explain details of agreement<br>• Provision for modification of terms of the Agreement<br>• Agreement signed in the community at a mass meeting | • Flexibility in terms of Agreement |
| 10 | Preparation of detailed design, materials requirement, cost estimate | • Done by Agency staff (or consultants) in office using standard procedures | • Design according to standards, but with drawings and explanation that can be understood by community<br>• Transparent materials estimation<br>• Transparent costs estimation | • Methods for presenting engineering design concepts in simple terms<br>• Transparent materials and costs estimating formats |
| 11 | Presentation of designs and cost estimates to communities | • Not done | • Presented, explained and discussed<br>• Adjustments made by community<br>• Copy of design, materials quantities and cost estimates given to community | • Additional step<br>• Change in attitude of technical staff to share and explain engineering knowledge<br>• Adequate time |
| 12 | Training to WUSC in management of construction | • Not done (Agency manages construction) | • Management training given to all members of WUSC on site | • Participatory training techniques |
| 13 | Procurement of materials | • Central or regional procurement | • Procurement as close as possible to point of use<br>• WUSC involved in tender appraisal<br>• Purchase accounts open to community | • Decentralised procurement<br>• Procedures to allow WUSC to appraise tenders<br>• Transparent accounting |
| 14 | Construction | • By contractor supervised by Agency staff | • By community with technical guidance and support from technical facilitator (WST) | • Abolition of contracting system<br>• Materials and financial advances to community for construction materials<br>• Training in management of construction WST full-time on site<br>• |
| 15 | Hygiene and water use education | • Lecturing style of teaching<br>• Limited target group (WUSC only) | • Participatory teaching materials and training methods<br>• Targeting effective motivators in village (village health volunteers, women's groups, youth volunteers, WUSC, etc.)<br>• Follow-up trainings | • Participatory training materials and methods<br>• Trained trainers<br>• Adequate time |

| | Activity | Implementor | Facilitator | Changes needed |
|---|---|---|---|---|
| 16 | Sanitation | ▪ Insisting that people (WUSC members) build latrines | ▪ Latrines built as a result of genuine understanding and demand | ▪ Hygiene and water use education<br>▪ Latrines not used as only targets and indicators of hygiene and sanitation coverage |
| 17 | Training of VMW | ▪ Lecturing style of teaching | ▪ Participatory training | ▪ Participatory training materials and methods |
| 18 | Training of WUSC for management of O&M | ▪ Lecturing style of teaching | ▪ Participatory training | ▪ Participatory training materials and methods |
| 19 | Completion ceremony | ▪ 'Hand-over' of scheme to users | ▪ Celebration of community's achievement in constructing their own system | ▪ Reorientation of concept of 'ownership' |
| 20 | O&M monitoring and follow-up support | ▪ By DWSO<br>▪ Not done until repair required | ▪ Regular visits by MST to ensure that WUSC and VMW are confident and functioning | ▪ Application of 1993 O&M Policy<br>▪ Budget allocation and staff |

## Abbreviations

**Abbreviations:**

| | |
|---|---|
| DDC | District Development Committee (appointed by elected District Assembly) |
| DE | District Engineer (employed by DWSO) |
| DWSS | Department of Water Supply & Sewerage |
| DWSO | District Water Supply Office (responsible to DWSS) |
| MST | Maintenance & Sanitation Technician (employed by DWSO) |
| O&M | Operation and maintenance |
| PRA | Participatory rural appraisal |
| VMW | Village Maintenance Worker (responsible to WUSC) |
| WST | Water & Sanitation Technician (employed by DWSO) |
| WUSC | Water User & Sanitation Committee (elected by community) |

## Progress

The Fourth Loan Project was agreed between the ADB and the Government of Nepal in November 1996, and work started in January 1997. The project is due for completion by mid-2001, with a mid-term review scheduled for the end of 1998.

Progress in the transition by the DWSS from implementor to facilitator includes the appointment of sociologists, the training of technical staff (engineers, overseers and technicians) in PRA methodologies and social preparation, and development of new procedures with information sheets in Nepali for distribution in villages. In addition DWSS has issued a directive that construction cannot be started until the preparation phase is completed. About four months is allowed for this phase, covered by Activities 8 to 12 in Table 1. DWSS has developed a strong support and monitoring programme to ensure that the facilitation process is followed. For the first time a budget allocation for social preparation work is included in the new Ninth Five Year Plan of His Majesty's Government of Nepal.

## References

Asian Development Bank, and Department of Water Supply and Sewerage (1996), *Fourth Rural Water Supply and Sanitation Sector Project: Final Report of the Project Preparation Technical Assistance*, ADB/DWSS (unpublished), Kathmandu.

IRC International Water & Sanitation Centre (1995), 'The Influence of Technology on Operation and Maintenance of Rural Water Supply Projects', in *Integrated Rural Water Management*, ed. WHO, Geneva.

Shrestha V.L. and Pyakural D.C. (1996), 'Community management and socialising engineers', in *Reaching the Unreached: Challenges for the 21st Century*, Proceedings of the 22nd WEDC Conference, J. Pickford *et al.* (eds), WEDC, Loughborough.

Appendices

# Appendix C: References and Bibliography

African Development Bank, 1990, *Environmental Sector Policy Paper*, African Development Bank.

Almedom, A., Blumenthal, U. and Manderson, L., 1997. *Hygiene Evaluation Procedures*. International Nutrition Foundation for Developing Countries, London.

American Society of Civil Engineers, 1996. *Hydrology Handbook* (2nd edition). ASCE Manuals and Reports on Engineering Practice, No.28. American Society of Civil Engineers, New York.

Asian Development Bank, 1992. *Guidelines for The Health Impact Assessment of Development Projects*, Office of the Environment, Asian Development Bank, Manila.

Asian Development Bank, 1993. *Environmental Assessment Requirements and Environmental Review Procedures of the Asian Development Bank*. Asian Development Bank, Manila.

Asian Development Bank, 1994. *Handbook for Incorporation of Social Dimensions in Projects*. Asian Development Bank, Manila.

Asian Development Bank, 1998.*Guidelines on the Use of Consultants by Asian Development Bank and its Borrowers*. Asian Development Bank, Manila

Banez-Ockelford, J., 1995. *Partners in Creative Training*. PACT/JSI, Phnom Penh, Cambodia.

Bolt, E. (Editor), 1994. *Together for Water and Sanitation: Tools to Apply a Gender Approach - The Asian Experience*. Occasional Paper Series No.24. IRC International Water and Sanitation Centre, The Hague.

Boot M.T., 1990. *Making the Links: Guidelines for Hygiene Education in Community Water Supply and Sanitation*, Occasional Paper Series Nos. 5. IRC International Water and Sanitation Centre, The Hague.

Boot, M.T., 1991. *Just Stir Gently: The way to mix hygiene education with water supply and sanitation*. Technical Paper Series No. 29. IRC International Water and Sanitation Centre, The Hague.

Boot, M.T. and Cairncross, S. (Editors), 1993. *Actions Speak: The study of hygiene behaviour in water and sanitation projects*. London School of Hygiene and Tropical Medicine and IRC International Water and Sanitation Centre, The Hague. .

Brassington, R., 1988. *Field Hydrogeology*. Geological Society of London Professional Handbook. Open University Press, Milton Keynes, UK.

Bureau of Reclamation, U.S.A., 1997. *Water Measurement Manual* (Third Edition). Bureau of Reclamation, United States Department of the Interior, in co-operation with the U S Department of Agriculture. United States Government Printing Office, Pittsburgh, USA

Cairncross, S. Carruthers I., Curtis D., Feachem R., Bradley D., Baldwin G., 1980. *Evaluation for Village Water Supply Planning*. John Wiley & Sons, Chichester.

Cairncross, S. and Feachem, R., 1986. *Small Water Supplies*. Ross Bulletin No.10. The Ross Institute of Tropical Hygiene, London.

Cairncross, S. and Feachem, R., 1993. *Environmental Health Engineering in the Tropics*. John Wiley & Sons, Chichester, UK.

Cairncross S., and Kochar V., 1994. *Studying Hygiene Behaviour. Methods, Issues and Experiences*. Sage Publications, London.

Calow R.C., Robins N.S., MacDonald A.M., Macdonald D.M.J., Gibbs B.R., Orpen W.R.G., Mtembezeka P., Andrews A.J. and Appiah S.O., 1997. 'Groundwater management in drought prone areas of Africa', *International Journal of Water Resources Development*, 13, 2, pp.241-261

Chambers, R., 1993. *Challenging the Professions*. IT Publications, London.

Chandler, C.G., 1985. *Achieving Success in Community Water Supply and Sanitation Projects*. SEARO Regional Health Papers No.9. WHO, New Delhi.

Colin, J., 1999. *VLOM for Rural Water Supply: Lessons from Experience*. Task No.162, WELL, London and Loughborough.

Cotton, A., Pintelon, L., Janssens, J. and Gelders, L., 1994. *Tools for the Assessment of Operation and Maintenance Status of Water Supplies*. WHO, Geneva.

Cullivan, D., Tippett, B., Edwards, D.B., Rosenweig, F. and McCaffery, J., 1988. *Guidelines for*

Appendices

*Institutional Assessment: Water and Wastewater Institutions.* WASH Technical Report No.37. WASH, Washington D.C.

Davis, J. and Brikke, F., 1995. *Making your water supply work: Operation and maintenance of small water supply systems.* Occasional Paper Series No. 29. IRC International Water and Sanitation Centre, The Hague.

Davis, J., Garvey, G. and Wood, M., 1993. *Developing and Managing Community Water Supplies.* Oxfam Development Guidelines No.8. Oxfam, Oxford.

Dublin (1992) *The Dublin Statement and Report of the Conference,* International Conference on Water and the Environment: Development issues for the 21$^{st}$ Century, 26-31 January 1992, Dublin, Ireland.

Eade, D. and Williams, S. (Editors), 1995. *The Oxfam Handbook of Development and Relief,* Oxfam, Oxford.

Edwards, D.B., Salt, E. and Rosenweig, F., 1992. *Making Choices for Sectoral Organization in Water and Sanitation.* WASH Reprint: Technical Report No. 74. Environmental Health Project (formerly WASH), Washington D.C.

Edwards, D.B., Rosenweig, F. and Salt, E., 1993. *Designing and Implementing Decentralisation Programs in the Water and Sanitation Sector.* WASH Technical Report No.89. WASH, Washington D.C.

Environmental Health Project, 1997. *Better Sanitation Programming: A UNICEF Handbook.* EHP Applied Study No.5. Environmental Health Project, Washington D.C.

Evans, P., 1992. *Paying the Piper: An overview of community financing of water and sanitation.* Occasional Paper Series. IRC International Water and Sanitation Centre, The Hague,.

FAO, 1995. *Water sector policy review and strategy formulation: A general framework.* FAO Land and Water Bulletin No.3. FAO, Rome.

Freeze R.A. and Cherry J. A., 1979. *Groundwater.* Prentice Hall, New Jersey.

Frelick, G., and Fry, S., 1990. *Training on Hygiene Education.* WASH Reprint: Technical Report No 60. Environmental Health Project (formerly WASH), Washington D.C.

Gajanayake, S. and Gajanayake, J., 1993. *Community Empowerment: A Participatory Training Manual on Community Project Development.* PACT Publications, New York.

Good, A., 1996. 'Social Issues in NGO Water Projects' in I. Smout (Editor), *Water and NGOs: Proceedings of an ODA workshop.* WEDC, Loughborough University, Loughborough.

Gosling, L. and Edwards, W.M., 1995. *Toolkits: A Practical Guide to Assessment, Monitoring, Review and Evaluation.* Save the Children Development Manual No.5. Save the Children, London.

Gunston, H.M., 1998. *Field Hydrology in Tropical Countries.* IT Publications, London.

Hamill L. and Bell F.G., 1986. *Groundwater Resource Development.* Butterworths, Sevenoaks, UK.

Hamilton, D. and Gaertner, U., 1991. *Goal Oriented Project Planning: An Introduction to the Methodology.* UNDP Office for Project Services, GTZ, Manila.

Handy, C., 1993. *Understanding Organizations.* Penguin Books, London.

International Labour Office, 1993. *How to select and use consultants: A client's guide.* ILO, Geneva.

IRC and NETWAS (Editors), 1994. *Working with Women and Men on Water and Sanitation: An African Field Guide.* Occasional Paper Series. IRC International Water and Sanitation Centre, The Hague.

Jordan, T., 1984. *A Handbook of Gravity-Flow Water Systems.* Intermediate Technology Publications, London.

Kamminga, E., 1991. *Economic Benefits from Improved Rural Water Supply: A review with a focus on women.* IRC Occasional Paper. IRC International Water and Sanitation Centre, The Hague.

Kjellerup, B. and Ockelford, J., 1993. 'Handpump standardization in Cambodia' in *Waterlines* 12 (No.1), IT Publications, London.

Lerner D.N., Issar A.S. and Simmers I., 1990. *Groundwater recharge.* International Contributions to Hydrogeology No.8. International Association of Hydrogeologists, Kenilworth, UK.

**Appendices**

Linney, B., 1995. *People, Pictures and Power: People-centred visual aids for development.* MacMillan and TALC, London.

Linsley, R.K., 1981. *Hydrology for Engineers* (3rd edition). McGraw Hill, New York.

Listorti J.A., *Environmental Health Components for Water Supply, Sanitation, and Urban Projects.* World Bank Technical Paper Number 121. The World Bank, Washington, D.C.

Lutz W., Chalmers, Hepburn and Lockerbie, 1992. *Health & Community Surveys.* Volumes I & II. Macmillan, London.

Mbewe, I.J. and Sutton, S., 1999. 'Under-estimated potential of traditional water sources?' in J. Pickford (Editor), *Integrated development for water supply and sanitation.* Proceedings of 25th WEDC Conference, Addis Ababa. WEDC, Loughborough.

Miloradov, M. and Marjanovic, P., 1998. *Guidelines for conducting water resources assessment.* Studies and reports in hydrology. UNESCO Publishing, Paris.

Morgan D.L., 1988. *Focus Groups as Qualitative Research.* Sage Publications, Newbury Park, CA, USA.

Morgan, P., 1990. *Rural Water Supplies and Sanitation.* MacMillan Education Ltd, London.

Mpumalanga Workshop, 1999. *Financing of Community Water and Sanitation Services: The Mpumalanga Statement.* DWAF, Mvula Trust, WSP-ESA, UNICEF, DFID. http://www.africanwater.org/mpumalanga_statement.htm

Narayan, D., 1993. *Participatory Evaluation: Tools for managing change in water and sanitation.* World Bank Technical Paper No.207. World Bank, Washington D.C.

Narayan, D. and Srinivasan, L., 1994. *Participatory Development Toolkit: Training materials for agencies and communities.* World Bank, Washington D.C.

Noppen, D. (Editor), 1996. *Village Level Operation and Maintenance of Handpumps: Experiences from Karonga, Malawi.* Project and Programme Papers. IRC International Water and Sanitation Centre, The Hague.

Ockelford, J., 1996. 'Technical and Management Issues' in I. Smout (Editor) *Water and NGOs: Proceedings of an ODA Workshop.* Loughborough University, Loughborough.

Ockelford, J. and Shrestha, V., 1998. Implementor or Facilitator? Achieving Community Management in Nepal. In: J. Pickford (Editor), 24th WEDC Conference: Sanitation and Water for All. WEDC, Islamabad, pp. 110-113.

Pickford, J., 1995. *Low-Cost Sanitation: A survey of practical experience.* IT Publications, London.

Pickford, J. (Editor), 1998. *Sanitation and Water for All: Proceedings of the 24th WEDC Conference.* WEDC, Loughborough.

Reinke, W.A., Stanton, B.F., Roberts, L. and Newman, J., 1993. *Rapid Assessment for Decision Making: Efficient Methods for Data Collection and Analysis.* WASH Field Report No.391. WASH, Washington D.C.

Roark, P., Hodgkin, J. and Wyatt, A., 1993. *Models of Management Systems for the Operation and Maintenance of Rural Water Supply and Sanitation Facilities.* Environmental Health Project/ WHO, Washington D.C.

Saywell, D., 1999. 'Pollution from on-site sanitation - the risk? What risks?' *Waterlines,* 17, No.4. IT Publications, London.

Schaefer M., 1993, *Health, Environment and Development: Approaches to Drafting County-Level Strategies for Human Well Being under Agenda 21.* WHO, Geneva.

Slocum, R., Wichhart, L., Rocheleau, D. and Thomas-Slayter, B. (Editors), 1995. *Power, Process and Participation: Tools for Change.* IT Publications, London.

Struckmeier W. F. and Margat J., 1995. *Hydrogeological maps: A guide and a standard legend.* International Contributions to Hydrogeology No.17. International Association of Hydrogeologists, Kenilworth, UK.

Therkildsen, O., 1988. *Watering White Elephants?* Scandinavian Institute of African Studies, Uppsala.

Thomas-Slayter B., Esser A.L. and Shields M.D., 1993. *Tools of Gender Analysis: A Guide to Field Methods for Bringing Gender into Sustainable Resource Management,* ECOGEN Research Project, International Development Program, Clark University, Worcester, MA, USA.

**Appendices**

Todd, D.K., 1980. *Groundwater Hydrology* (2nd edition). John Wiley, New York.

Tomaro, J.B. and Wall, R.E., 1991. *Technical Assistance to the African Development Bank: Development of Guidelines for Project Preparation and Appraisal in Water Supply and Sanitation*. WASH Field Report No. 333. WASH, Washington D.C.

Twort A.C., Law F.M. and Crowley F.W., 1985. *Water Supply*. Edward Arnold, London

Wakeman, W., 1995. *Gender Issues Sourcebook for Water and Sanitation Projects*. UNDP-World Bank Water & Sanitation Program, Washington D.C.

Walton W.C., 1970. *Groundwater Resource Evaluation*. McGraw-Hill, New York.

WASH, 1987, *Guidelines for Designing a Hygiene Education Programme in Water Supply and Sanitation for Regional/District Level Personnel*. WASH Field Report 218. Washington D.C.

Water Supply & Sanitation Collaborative Council, 2000. *Vision 21: A Shared Vision for Hygiene, Sanitation and Water Supply and a Framework for Action*. WSSCC, Geneva.

Watt S.B. and Wood W.E., 1979. Hand Dug Wells and Their Construction. IT Publications, London.

WELL for DFID, 1998. *Guidance Manual on Water Supply and Sanitation Programmes*. WEDC, Loughborough.

Werner, D. and Bower, B., 1982. *Helping Health Workers Learn*. The Hesperian Foundation, Palo Alto, California.

Whyte, A., 1986. *Guidelines for planning community participation activities in water supply and sanitation projects*. WHO Offset Publication No.96. WHO, Geneva.

Wijk-Sijbesma, C. van, 1985. *Participation of Women in Water Supply and Sanitation*. Technical Paper No. 22, 22. International Reference Centre for Community Water Supply and Sanitation, The Hague.

Wijk-Sijbesma, C. van, 1998. *Gender in Water Resources Management, Water Supply and Sanitation*. Technical Paper Series. IRC International Water and Sanitation Centre, The Hague.

Wilson, E.M., 1990. *Engineering hydrology* (4th edition). Macmillan, Basingstoke, UK.

Wood, S., Sawyer, R. and Simpson-Hebert, M., 1998. *PHAST Step-by-step Guide: A participatory approach for the control of diarrhoeal disease*. WHO, Geneva.

World Health Organisation, 1985. *Guidelines for Drinking-Water Quality: Vol.3 Drinking-water quality control in small-community supplies*. WHO, Geneva.

World Health Organisation, 1993. *Guidelines for drinking-water quality: Volume 1 Recommendations*. WHO, Geneva.

World Health Organisation, 1994. *Financial management of water supply and sanitation*. WHO, Geneva.

World Health Organisation and UNICEF, 1998. Water Supply and Sanitation Sector Monitoring Report, World Health Organisation, Geneva.

World Meteorological Organisation, 1994. *Guide to Hydrological Practices: Data acquisition and processing, analysis, forecasting and other applications* (5th edition). WMO No.68. World Meteorological Organisation, Geneva.

**Appendices**

www.ingramcontent.com/pod-product-compliance
Lightning Source LLC
Chambersburg PA
CBHW080952050426
42334CB00057B/2607